BENNY HINN

Lamb of GOD

YESTERDAY

TODAY & FOREVER

CLARION CALL MARKETING

LAMB OF GOD: YESTERDAY, TODAY, & FOREVER

Published by:
Clarion Call Marketing, Inc.
Dallas, Texas

ISBN: 1-59574-000-7

www.BennyHinn.org

Printed in the United States of America.
08   07   06   05   04   1   2   3   4   5   6

CONTENTS

THE INVITATION OF THE AGES

Behold the Lamb of God, which taketh away the sin of the world.

—JOHN 1:29

WHY DID JESUS CHRIST DIE on the cross? What caused the Son of Man to do the unthinkable, to give His life as a substitute for each of us?

Questions about Jesus Christ, especially about His death, burial, and resurrection, continue to this day. I've written this book specifically to respond to the many inquiries about Jesus Christ that men, women, and children around the globe are struggling to answer, now more than ever. If anything, the increased shaking of the world's financial, political, and territorial foundations are forcing even more people to look to the Cross for solutions. The timing couldn't be better.

I understand the volume of questions, because I've spent a lifetime seeking the same answers. And the Cross is simply not taught much in today's churches. The response from my book *The Blood* helped me understand to an even greater extent how hungry people really are to know more about this momentous, historical, spiritual, and celebrated event that is often simply not discussed or taught. Why did Jesus Christ die on the cross?

The story of Christ's crucifixion has perhaps become so familiar to both believers and nonbelievers that it has often lost its ability to inspire grief or even to stir any great emotion. Somehow, through the centuries, mankind has attempted to sanitize history's pivotal moment. We've taken away the horrible public shame and the smashing blows of the whip. We've attempted to avoid the savage thrust of the spear into Jesus's side. In so doing, too often the Easter story ignores God's supernatural love as it was poured out among mankind.

In the world today there are so many questions about the Cross, yet I believe it is time for men, women, and children everywhere to be told about the triumph of God's plan, expressed two centuries ago through the Holy Spirit–inspired word of John's Gospel: *"Behold, the Lamb of God, which taketh away the sin of the world."*

HISTORY'S TURNING POINT

No matter how people get to the place of seeking deeper answers about the death, burial, and resurrection of Jesus Christ, they have arrived at the place of all answers and the Answer. Everything in history, before and afterward, points toward Calvary's cross. History is, after all, HIS-story. Mankind, almost universally, uses the Gregorian (and sometimes the Julian) calendar which separates time by BC (before Christ) and AD (an abbreviation for *anno Domini* in Latin, which translates "in the year of our Lord," referring to the approximate birth year of Jesus Christ).

History is, after all, HIS-story.

Even politically correct attempts to translate BC to BCE (before the common era) and AD to CE (common era) have not been able to diminish the fact that the Savior stands boldly as the center point for all mankind.

Certainly, the Bible points to the centrality of Christ Jesus. People sometimes talk about the differences in the God of the Old Testament and the God of the New Testament. But Christianity teaches that the God of the Old Testament *is* the God of the New Testament. God may have revealed Himself to us in progressive stages, but He is eternal and unchangeable.

Some people seem to misapprehend the relationship between the Old and New Testaments, as if there is some major difference between the two. Christ Jesus, however, said that He came to fulfill the law, not to abolish it.

The Bible doesn't begin with the New Testament. It is an integrated document from Genesis through Revelation. Virtually every page of the Old Testament points to the New.

"In the beginning was the Word," the Gospel of John begins, referring to Jesus as the Word, *"and the Word was with God, and the Word was God"* (1:1). Having established Christ's exalted place in all eternity, John—under the inspiration of the Holy Spirit—continues to pen these powerful truths: *"The same was in the beginning with God. All things were made by him; and without him was not any thing made that was made. In him was life; and the life was the light of men"* (1:2–4).

But why would Jesus do what He did? What caused Him to leave heaven's splendor to be born a baby in Bethlehem? What could have possibly motivated Him to endure a life of temptation and peril as He sought to call, disciple, and prepare a handful of followers who would eventually be sent out to shake the world's traditions to the core and bring hope and healing to the masses? Why would He willingly go through the shame and vile, inhuman treatment at the hands of people who didn't (or couldn't) grasp the historic event in which they were participating? What is the true story behind His death? What happened afterward that has eternal consequences for you and me?

As you look for answers, dear reader, gaze toward the Christ of Calvary, for that is the central point of all truth, wisdom, and knowledge. It is that truth that has changed the world's hardest men and women into God's most effective witnesses. It is that truth that has played an important role in the panorama of people who have yearned to be free from totalitarianism and human bondage. It has changed the course of history, kings, and great military leaders.

Everything before and after Calvary points to what the Savior did on the cross. Because of His sacrifice, and so much more, we have the Answer to the most pressing, troubling, life-changing questions you will ever have. He is the blessed Christ of the Cross, and what an eternal difference He has already made in the life of every believer. That's why we can sing:

> On a hill far away stood an old rugged cross,
> The emblem of suff'ring and shame;
> And I love that old cross where the dearest and best
> For a world of lost sinners was slain.
>
> So I'll cherish the old rugged cross,
> Till my trophies at last I lay down.
> I will cling to the old rugged cross,
> And exchange it some day for a crown.[1]

1

THE LAMB OF GOD:
332 PROPHECIES

To him give all the prophets witness, that through his name whosoever believeth in him shall receive remission of sins.

—ACTS 10:43

HE OLD TESTAMENT WAS GIVEN by the Holy Spirit to the prophets of old and was completed approximately four hundred fifty years before Christ Jesus was born in Bethlehem. This is especially exciting for Bible scholars as they understand how more than three hundred prophecies, many in graphic detail, were meticulously predicted throughout the Old Testament, then astonishingly fulfilled one by one through the birth, life, crucifixion, burial, resurrection, and ascension of only one person in all of history, Jesus Christ.

When studying the New Testament, I believe a clear understanding of the Old Testament is vital, since the Old Testament is incomplete without the New. It's like this: The New Testament in the Old is concealed, and the Old in the New is revealed. It's imperative that you have both!

Let's talk about how the Old and New are amazingly complete as they announce and fulfill the messianic prophecies. Scholars cite the chances of one person fulfilling a mere eight of the messianic prophecies as one in 100,000,000,000,000,000. Josh McDowell writes of these amazing odds:

> For one person to fulfill 48 of these prophecies, the number becomes staggering—1 chance in 10 to the 157th power (1 with 157 zeros after it). Add to that the 250 other prophecies and it becomes impossible for any other person except Jesus to ever fit that particular sequence of time and events.[1]

Prophecies and Fulfillments

There are many wonderful predictions in the Old Testament which offered great detail in pointing toward Jesus Christ's birth, life, death, burial, resurrection, and ascension. For additional study, I will give a more complete list of 332 of these messianic prophecies at the end of this chapter. Here are a few that I've detailed:

The Messiah would rise from Abraham's lineage. This was outlined in Genesis 18:18 (written approximately fourteen hundred years before Christ's birth): *"Seeing that Abraham shall surely become a great and mighty nation, and all the nations of the earth shall be blessed in him?"* (Also read Genesis 12:3.)

This is also a matter of historic certainty, as described in Acts 3:25: *"Ye are the children of the prophets, and of the covenant which God made with our fathers, saying unto Abraham, And in thy seed shall all the kindreds of the earth be blessed."* (Also read Galatians 3:8.)

In addition to Abraham's bloodline, Jesus would specifically descend from Abraham's son, Isaac. Genesis 17:19 explains: *"And God said, Sarah thy wife shall bear thee a son indeed; and thou shalt call his* name Isaac: and I will establish my covenant with him for an everlasting covenant, and with his seed after him."

Matthew 1:1–2 and 15–17 points to the fulfillment:

> The book of the generation of Jesus Christ, the son of David, the son of Abraham. Abraham begat Isaac; and Isaac begat Jacob; and Jacob begat Judas and his brethren;…and Eleazar begat Matthan; and Matthan begat Jacob; and Jacob begat Joseph the husband of Mary, of whom was born Jesus, who is called Christ. So all the generations from Abraham to David are fourteen generations.

Also, the Messiah would be a direct descendant of Abraham's grandson and Isaac's son Jacob, not his other son Esau. Numbers 24:16–17 points out:

> He hath said, which heard the words of God, and knew the knowledge of the most High, which saw the vision of the Almighty, falling into a trance, but having his eyes open: I shall see him, but not now: I shall behold him, but not nigh: there shall come a Star out of Jacob, and a Sceptre shall rise out of Israel, and shall smite the corners of Moab, and destroy all the children of Sheth.

This was clearly fulfilled, as described in Luke 3:23, 34:

> And Jesus himself began to be about thirty years of age, being (as was supposed) the son of Joseph, which was the son of Heli,…which was the son of Jacob, which was the son of Isaac, which was the son of Abraham, which was the son of Thara, which was the son of Nachor.

The Christ would come from Judah, one of Israel's twelve tribes. Genesis 49:10 (written approximately 1400 BC) describes the lineage this way: *"The sceptre shall not depart from Judah, nor a lawgiver from between his feet, until Shiloh come; and unto him shall the gathering of the people be."* This exact line of genealogy is detailed in Luke 3:23, 33:

> And Jesus himself began to be about thirty years of age, being (as was supposed) the son of Joseph, which was the son of Heli,…which was the son of Aminadab, which was the son of Aram, which was the son of Esrom, which was the son of Phares, which was the son of Juda [Judah].

The specific place of the Savior's birth was predicted to be the small village of Bethlehem. The prophet Micah (who wrote his Holy Spirit–inspired prediction sometime between 750 and 686 years before Christ) points to the lineage from the tribe of Judah, but he further describes the small town, located a little over five miles southwest of Jerusalem, that would be the Messiah's birthplace: *"But thou, Bethlehem Ephratah, though thou be little among the thousands of Judah, yet out of thee shall he come forth unto me that is to be ruler in Israel; whose goings forth have been from of old, from everlasting"* (Micah 5:2).

Matthew 2:1 reveals the exact prophetic fulfillment, even though the parents of baby Jesus actually lived in Nazareth, a village then consisting of probably only a dozen or so families: *"Now when Jesus was born in Bethlehem of Judaea in the days of Herod the king, behold, there came wise men from the east to Jerusalem."*

Christ Jesus would be born supernaturally of a virgin. Isaiah 7:13–14 (Bible scholars and historians point to these words being written sometime between 701 and 681 BC):

> And he said, Hear ye now, O house of David; Is it a small thing for you to weary men, but will ye weary my God also? Therefore the

*Lord himself shall give you a sign; Behold, a virgin shall conceive,
and bear a son, and shall call his name Immanuel.*

Matthew 1:18 points to the amazing prediction that came true:
*"Now the birth of Jesus Christ was on this wise: When as his mother Mary
was espoused to Joseph, before they came together, she was found with child
of the Holy Ghost."*

**Joseph and Mary would be forced to flee with the Christ child
and relocate to Egypt for safety's sake.** Hosea 11:1 foretells: *"When
Israel was a child, then I loved him, and called my son out of Egypt."*

Matthew Henry, the noted Bible scholar, wrote:

> These words are said to have been fulfilled in Christ, when,
> upon the death of Herod, he and his parents were "called out
> of Egypt" (Mt. 2:15), so that the words have a double aspect,
> speaking historically of the calling of Israel out of Egypt and
> prophetically of the bringing of Christ thence; and the former
> was a type of the latter.

Matthew 2:13–15 shares the fulfillment of this prediction:

> *And when they were departed, behold, the angel of the Lord appeareth
> to Joseph in a dream, saying, Arise, and take the young child and his
> mother, and flee into Egypt, and be thou there until I bring thee word:
> for Herod will seek the young child to destroy him. When he arose, he
> took the young child and his mother by night, and departed into Egypt:
> And was there until the death of Herod: that it might be fulfilled which
> was spoken of the Lord by the prophet, saying, Out of Egypt have I
> called my son.*

When He began His public ministry, Jesus would minister throughout Galilee, mostly in the area of the Sea of Galilee and the Jordan River.

Isaiah 9:1–2 states:

> *Nevertheless the dimness shall not be such as was in her vexation, when at the first he lightly afflicted the land of Zebulun and the land of Naphtali, and afterward did more grievously afflict her by the way of the sea, beyond Jordan, in Galilee of the nations. The people that walked in darkness have seen a great light: they that dwell in the land of the shadow of death, upon them hath the light shined.*

In an astounding parallel, Matthew 4:12–17 describes the actual locations of Christ's ministry:

> *Now when Jesus had heard that John was cast into prison, he departed into Galilee; and leaving Nazareth, he came and dwelt in Capernaum, which is upon the sea coast, in the borders of Zabulon [Zebulun] and Nephthalim [Naphtali]: That it might be fulfilled which was spoken by Esaias [Isaiah] the prophet, saying, the land of Zabulon, and the land of Nephthalim, by the way of the sea, beyond Jordan, Galilee of the Gentiles; the people which sat in darkness saw great light; and to them which sat in the region and shadow of death light is sprung up. From that time Jesus began to preach.*

Even though Christ came from Jewish lineage, it was predicted without reservation that He would be rejected by His own people.

Isaiah 53:1–4 describes this rejection succinctly:

> *Who hath believed our report? and to whom is the arm of the LORD revealed? For he shall grow up before him as a tender plant, and as a*

root out of a dry ground: he hath no form nor comeliness; and when we shall see him, there is no beauty that we should desire him. He is despised and rejected of men; a man of sorrows, and acquainted with grief: and we hid as it were our faces from him; he was despised, and we esteemed him not. Surely he hath borne our griefs, and carried our sorrows: yet we did esteem him stricken, smitten of God, and afflicted.

In John 1:10–11, this historic fact is candidly stated: *"He was in the world, and the world was made by him, and the world knew him not. He came unto his own, and his own received him not."*

Jesus, from the lineage of Jesse, King David's father, would display unusual wisdom and character. Isaiah 11:1–2 offers the specific prophecy:

And there shall come forth a rod out of the stem of Jesse, and a Branch shall grow out of his roots: And the spirit of the LORD shall rest upon him, the spirit of wisdom and understanding, the spirit of counsel and might, the spirit of knowledge and of the fear of the LORD.

Luke 2:52 mirrors that prediction: *"And Jesus increased in wisdom and stature, and in favour with God and man."*

Jesus would enter Jerusalem triumphantly on a young donkey. Zechariah 9:9–10 (written between 520 and 518 BC) points to that day:

Rejoice greatly, O daughter of Zion; shout, O daughter of Jerusalem: behold, thy King cometh unto thee: he is just, and having salvation; lowly, and riding upon an ass, and upon a colt the foal of an ass. And I will cut off the chariot from Ephraim, and the horse from

Jerusalem, and the battle bow shall be cut off: and he shall speak
peace unto the heathen: and his dominion shall be from sea even to
sea, and from the river even to the ends of the earth.

John's gospel, written a half century later and recorded in chapter
12, verses 12 through 16 speaks of the fulfillment:

On the next day much people that were come to the feast, when
they heard that Jesus was coming to Jerusalem, took branches of
palm trees, and went forth to meet him, and cried, Hosanna:
Blessed is the King of Israel that cometh in the name of the Lord.
And Jesus, when he had found a young ass, sat thereon; as it is
written, Fear not, daughter of Sion [Zion]: behold, thy King
cometh, sitting on an ass's colt. These things understood not his
disciples at the first: but when Jesus was glorified, then remembered
they that these things were written of him, and that they had done
these things unto him.

The Savior would be betrayed for thirty pieces of silver. The
prophet Zechariah gave the specific amount: "And I said unto them, If
ye think good, give me my price; and if not, forbear. So they weighed for my
price thirty pieces of silver" (11:12).

Matthew 26:14–16 recorded the actual deed and amount:

Then one of the twelve, called Judas Iscariot, went unto the chief
priests, and said unto them, What will ye give me, and I will deliver
him unto you? And they covenanted with him for thirty pieces of
silver. And from that time he sought opportunity to betray him.

The fate of the blood money was foretold. Zechariah (written
between 520 and 518 BC) told how that silver would be returned by

the betrayer and eventually used to buy a potter's field: *"And the* LORD *said unto me, Cast it unto the potter: a goodly price that I was prised [prized] at of them. And I took the thirty pieces of silver, and cast them to the potter in the house of the* LORD*"* (Zechariah 11:13).

Matthew 27:3–10 gives a picture-perfect account of what actually happened to the man whose name still epitomizes betrayal and deceit:

> *Then Judas, which had betrayed him, when he saw that he was condemned, repented himself, and brought again the thirty pieces of silver to the chief priests and elders, saying, I have sinned in that I have betrayed the innocent blood. And they said, What is that to us? see thou to that. And he cast down the pieces of silver in the temple, and departed, and went and hanged himself. And the chief priests took the silver pieces, and said, It is not lawful for to put them into the treasury, because it is the price of blood. And they took counsel, and bought with them the potter's field, to bury strangers in. Wherefore that field was called, The field of blood, unto this day. Then was fulfilled that which was spoken by Jeremy [Jeremiah] the prophet, saying, And they took the thirty pieces of silver, the price of him that was valued, whom they of the children of Israel did value; and gave them for the potter's field, as the Lord appointed me.*

Jesus would be accused by false witnesses. Psalm 35:11 foretold, *"False witnesses did rise up; they laid to my charge things that I knew not."* Likewise, Psalm 109:2 relates: *"For the mouth of the wicked and the mouth of the deceitful are opened against me: they have spoken against me with a lying tongue."* A thousand years later, not only did the chief priests actually seek false witnesses against Christ Jesus (Matthew 26:59), but though many false witnesses came, they found none that could agree (Matthew 26:60), in what most historians and Bible scholars say was an illegal trial and desperate miscarriage of justice.

Christ would stand silent when accused during His trial. Isaiah (written between 701 and 681 BC) gave very explicit word pictures:

> *He was oppressed, and he was afflicted, yet he opened not his mouth: he is brought as a lamb to the slaughter, and as a sheep before her shearers is dumb, so he openeth not his mouth. (Isaiah 53:7)*

Matthew 26:62–63 points to this exact incident:

> *And the high priest arose, and said unto him, Answerest thou nothing? what is it which these witness against thee? But Jesus held his peace. And the high priest answered and said unto him, I adjure thee by the living God, that thou tell us whether thou be the Christ, the Son of God.*

Jesus would offer Himself as a willing sacrifice for the sins of mankind. Isaiah 53:4–6 offers this startling passage:

> *Surely he hath borne our griefs, and carried our sorrows: yet we did esteem him stricken, smitten of God, and afflicted. But he was wounded for our transgressions, he was bruised for our iniquities: the chastisement of our peace was upon him; and with his stripes we are healed. All we like sheep have gone astray; we have turned every one to his own way; and the LORD hath laid on him the iniquity of us all.*

Matthew 8:16–17, written nearly seven hundred years after Isaiah's prediction, points to Christ's sacrifice and the prediction:

> *When the even was come, they brought unto him many that were possessed with devils: and he cast out the spirits with his word, and healed all that were sick: That it might be fulfilled which was spoken*

by Esaias [Isaiah] the prophet, saying, Himself took our infirmities,
and bare our sicknesses.

The perfect Savior would be crucified with common criminals.
Isaiah 53:11–12 makes this prediction:

He shall see of the travail of his soul, and shall be satisfied: by his
knowledge shall my righteous servant justify many; for he shall bear
their iniquities. Therefore will I divide him a portion with the great, and
he shall divide the spoil with the strong; because he hath poured out his
soul unto death: and he was numbered with the transgressors; and he
bare the sin of many, and made intercession for the transgressors.

Mark 15:25–28 verifies what happened nearly seven hundred years
after Isaiah's prediction:

And it was the third hour, and they crucified him. And the super-
scription of his accusation was written over, THE KING OF THE
JEWS. And with him they crucify two thieves; the one on his right
hand, and the other on his left. And the scripture was fulfilled,
which saith, And he was numbered with the transgressors.

And while we are looking at this passage of Scripture, notice how
the Lord Jesus interceded for one of the thieves, as predicted seven
centuries before through Isaiah when the prophet wrote: "And he was
numbered with the transgressors; and he bare the sin of many, and made
intercession for the transgressors" (Isaiah 53:12). This was fulfilled
completely, as recorded in Luke 23:39–43:

And one of the malefactors which were hanged railed on him, saying,
If thou be Christ, save thyself and us. But the other answering

11

rebuked him, saying, Dost not thou fear God, seeing thou art in the same condemnation? And we indeed justly; for we receive the due reward of our deeds: but this man hath done nothing amiss. And he said unto Jesus, Lord, remember me when thou comest into thy kingdom. And Jesus said unto him, Verily I say unto thee, to day shalt thou be with me in paradise.

David the psalmist pointed to the fact that the Messiah's hands and feet would be pierced. This is especially unusual because during David's day, the Jews executed their criminals by stoning. Crucifixion became historically a Greek and Roman custom, but those empires didn't even exist when David penned these words (a millennium before the actual piercing):

My strength is dried up like a potsherd; and my tongue cleaveth to my jaws; and thou hast brought me into the dust of death. For dogs have compassed me: the assembly of the wicked have inclosed me: they pierced my hands and my feet. I may tell all my bones: they look and stare upon me. (Psalm 22:15–17)

This prophecy was fulfilled and proven to Thomas, the most doubting of the Savior's disciples, as recorded in John 20:24–28:

But Thomas, one of the twelve, called Didymus, was not with them when Jesus came. The other disciples therefore said unto him, We have seen the Lord. But he said unto them, Except I shall see in his hands the print of the nails, and put my finger into the print of the nails, and thrust my hand into his side, I will not believe. And after eight days again his disciples were within, and Thomas with them: then came Jesus, the doors being shut, and stood in the midst, and said, Peace be unto you. Then saith he to Thomas, Reach hither thy finger, and behold my hands; and reach hither thy hand, and thrust it into my side: and be not faithless, but believing. And Thomas answered and said unto him, My Lord and my God.

How much did seeing the scars change Thomas's life? Historians almost universally agree that Thomas spent the rest of his life preaching the gospel and founding churches, and then was reportedly martyred in India.

Christ would be reviled, mocked, and insulted by the people. Psalm 22:6–8 gives this glimpse:

But I am a worm, and no man; a reproach of men, and despised of the people. All they that see me laugh me to scorn: they shoot out the lip, they shake the head, saying, He trusted on the LORD that he would deliver him: let him deliver him, seeing he delighted in him.

Matthew 27:39–42, written a thousand years afterward, graphically portrays what happened on the cross:

And they that passed by reviled him, wagging their heads, and saying, Thou that destroyest the temple, and buildest it in three days, save thyself. If thou be the Son of God, come down from the cross. Likewise also the chief priests mocking him, with the scribes and elders, said, He saved others; himself he cannot save. If he be the King of Israel, let him now come down from the cross, and we will believe him.

David details a specific liquid that would be offered to Christ Jesus during His time on the cross when He took our shame. Psalm 69:19–21 says:

*Thou hast known my reproach, and my shame, and my dishonour:
mine adversaries are all before thee. Reproach hath broken my
heart; and I am full of heaviness: and I looked for some to take pity,
but there was none; and for comforters, but I found none. They
gave me also gall for my meat; and in my thirst they gave me vinegar to drink.*

John 19:28–30 mirrors the drink that was offered:

*After this, Jesus knowing that all things were now accomplished,
that the scripture might be fulfilled, saith, I thirst. Now there was set
a vessel full of vinegar: and they filled a spunge with vinegar, and
put it upon hyssop, and put it to his mouth. When Jesus therefore
had received the vinegar, he said, It is finished.*

**The prophet Zechariah predicted that the Savior's side would be
pierced with a spear.** This prophecy, made sometime between 520 and
518 BC, is also unusual because it refers both to Christ's lineage and
where the piercing would take place:

*And I will pour upon the house of David, and upon the inhabitants
of Jerusalem, the spirit of grace and of supplications: and they shall
look upon me whom they have pierced, and they shall mourn for
him, as one mourneth for his only son, and shall be in bitterness for
him, as one that is in bitterness for his firstborn. (Zechariah 12:10)*

John 19:34–36 reveals the fulfillment:

*But one of the soldiers with a spear pierced his side, and forthwith
came there out blood and water. And he that saw it bare record, and
his record is true: and he knoweth that he saith true, that ye might*

believe. For these things were done, that the scripture should be fulfilled.

Another prediction from the psalmist told how the soldiers would cast lots for the Savior's clothing. Psalm 22:18–19 reveals: *"They part my garments among them, and cast lots upon my vesture. But be not thou far from me, O LORD: O my strength, haste thee to help me."*

Matthew 27:35–36 points to what happened nearly a millennium after the Holy Spirit inspired the shepherd David to pen those words: *"And they crucified him, and parted his garments, casting lots: that it might be fulfilled which was spoken by the prophet, They parted my garments among them, and upon my vesture did they cast lots."*

More specifically, David described how not one bone of Christ's body would be broken. Psalm 34:18–20 states:

> *The LORD is nigh unto them that are of a broken heart; and saveth such as be of a contrite spirit. Many are the afflictions of the righteous: but the LORD delivereth him out of them all. He keepeth all his bones: not one of them is broken.*

Amazingly, even after the torture before and during the crucifixion, John 19:31–33 describes what happened:

> *The Jews therefore, because it was the preparation, that the bodies should not remain upon the cross on the sabbath day, (for that sabbath day was an high day,) besought Pilate that their legs might be broken, and that they might be taken away. Then came the soldiers, and brake the legs of the first, and of the other which was crucified with him. But when they came to Jesus, and saw that he was dead already, they brake not his legs.*

Christ would be buried, not in a place of His own, but in a rich man's tomb. Isaiah 53:6–9 peers nearly seven hundred years into the future to describe how the burial ritual would unfold in a very uncommon manner:

All we like sheep have gone astray; we have turned every one to his own way; and the LORD hath laid on him the iniquity of us all. He was oppressed, and he was afflicted, yet he opened not his mouth: he is brought as a lamb to the slaughter, and as a sheep before her shearers is dumb, so he openeth not his mouth. He was taken from prison and from judgment: and who shall declare his generation? for he was cut off out of the land of the living: for the transgression of my people was he stricken. And he made his grave with the wicked, and with the rich in his death; because he had done no violence, neither was any deceit in his mouth.

Matthew 27:57–60 reveals what happened:

When the even was come, there came a rich man of Arimathaea, named Joseph, who also himself was Jesus' disciple: He went to Pilate, and begged the body of Jesus. Then Pilate commanded the body to be delivered. And when Joseph had taken the body, he wrapped it in a clean linen cloth, and laid it in his own new tomb, which he had hewn out in the rock: and he rolled a great stone to the door of the sepulchre, and departed.

In a most unusual prediction, David pointed to the Savior's resurrection after His death. Psalm 16:8–10 states:

I have set the LORD always before me: because he is at my right hand, I shall not be moved. Therefore my heart is glad, and my glory rejoiceth: my flesh also shall rest in hope. For thou wilt not leave my soul in hell; neither wilt thou suffer thine Holy One to see corruption.

Matthew 28:1–10 tells what took place a thousand years later:

In the end of the sabbath, as it began to dawn toward the first day of the week, came Mary Magdalene and the other Mary to see the sepulchre. And, behold, there was a great earthquake: for the angel of the Lord descended from heaven, and came and rolled back the stone from the door, and sat upon it. His countenance was like lightning, and his raiment white as snow: And for fear of him the keepers did shake, and became as dead men. And the angel answered and said unto the women, Fear not ye: for I know that ye seek Jesus, which was crucified. He is not here: for he is risen, as he said. Come, see the place where the Lord lay. And go quickly, and tell his disciples that he is risen from the dead; and, behold, he goeth before you into Galilee; there shall ye see him: lo, I have told you. And they departed quickly from the sepulchre with fear and great joy; and did run to bring his disciples word. And as they went to tell his disciples, behold, Jesus met them, saying, All hail. And they came and held him by the feet, and worshiped him. Then said Jesus unto them, Be not afraid: go tell my brethren that they go into Galilee, and there shall they see me.

The psalmist also foretold how Jesus Christ would ascend to heaven. Psalm 68:18–19 offers this vivid description:

Thou hast ascended on high, thou hast led captivity captive: thou hast received gifts for men; yea, for the rebellious also, that the LORD God might dwell among them. Blessed be the Lord, who daily loadeth us with benefits, even the God of our salvation.

Luke 24:50–52 is one of the Gospels' accounts of what happened in full view of the apostles:

> And he led them out as far as to Bethany, and he lifted up his
> hands, and blessed them. And it came to pass, while he blessed
> them, he was parted from them, and carried up into heaven. And
> they worshipped him, and returned to Jerusalem with great joy.

The Savior's message of salvation and hope would reach to the ends of the earth. Isaiah 49:6 (written between 701 and 681 BC) provides an unusual panorama of the coming world impact, not just to Christ's own people, the Jews, but to all cultures around the globe: *"And he said, It is a light thing that thou shouldest be my servant to raise up the tribes of Jacob, and to restore the preserved of Israel: I will also give thee for a light to the Gentiles, that thou mayest be my salvation unto the end of the earth."*

All the prophets throughout the Old Testament, from Genesis to Malachi, foretold vital information about the coming Messiah, Christ Jesus.

This message continues to unfold because Christianity is decidedly unique in all of history for its evangelistic outreach to the hearts of mankind, rather than through subversion and domination. Followers of Jesus believe that salvation, forgiveness of sins, and an eternity with the Father forever in heaven are available to "whosoever will," meaning anyone who accepts Jesus Christ as Savior. History continues to prove Isaiah's inspired prophecy as Acts 13:47 proclaims: *"For so hath the Lord commanded us, saying, I have set thee to be a light of the Gentiles, that thou shouldest be for salvation unto the ends of the earth."*

A FINAL NOTE

The profound message of the Cross has been examined and reexamined through many generations. Great artists and sculptors have tried to capture the impacting message of its truth in their work. The search continues to this day for revelation of a man, the Savior, who would give Himself to die in such a way.

Written in Acts is a rather startling passage:

> *How God anointed Jesus of Nazareth with the Holy Ghost and with power: who went about doing good, and healing all that were oppressed of the devil; for God was with him. And we are witnesses of all things which he did both in the land of the Jews, and in Jerusalem; whom they slew and hanged on a tree: Him God raised up the third day, and shewed him openly; Not to all the people, but unto witnesses chosen before of God, even to us, who did eat and drink with him after he rose from the dead. And he commanded us to preach unto the people, and to testify that it is he which was ordained of God to be the Judge of quick and dead. To him give all the prophets witness, that through his name whosoever believeth in him shall receive remission of sins.* (10:38–43)

All the prophets throughout the Old Testament, from Genesis to Malachi, foretold vital information about the coming Messiah, Christ Jesus. As mentioned in the first part of this chapter, it is mathematically impossible that one man could have fulfilled even a few of the specific prophecies, much less more than three hundred. Only on this one Person, in all of history, is the exact fulfillment of all these prophecies.

Christ Jesus, in fact, is the subject, goal, and center of all prophecy throughout the Old and New Testaments. He was what inspired the prophets through the centuries to testify beforehand of the birth, life, death, burial, and resurrection of the Savior.

Old Testament prophecies pointed forward to the Savior. When He came to earth, exactly as foretold, He then openly and candidly revealed to His followers, friends, and even enemies what had been written of Him.

> *While the Pharisees were gathered together, Jesus asked them, Saying, What think ye of Christ? whose son is he? They say unto him, The son of David. He saith unto them, How then doth David in spirit call him Lord, saying, The LORD said unto my Lord, Sit thou on my right hand, till I make thine enemies thy footstool? If David then call him Lord; how is he his son? And no man was able to answer him a word, neither durst any man from that day forth ask him any more questions.* (Matthew 22:41–46)

> *Then he said unto them, O fools, and slow of heart to believe all that the prophets have spoken: Ought not Christ to have suffered these things, and to enter into his glory? And beginning at Moses and all the prophets, he expounded unto them in all the scriptures the things concerning himself…. And he said unto them, These are the words which I spake unto you, while I was yet with you, that all things must be fulfilled, which were written in the law of Moses, and in the prophets, and in the psalms, concerning me. Then opened he their understanding, that they might understand the scriptures.* (Luke 24:25–27, 44–45)

Jesus spoke very pointedly to the unbelief of some listeners, and His words echo to our times: *"For had ye believed Moses, ye would have believed me: for he wrote of me. But if ye believe not his writings, how shall ye believe my words?"* (John 5:46–47).

More to the point, in Mark 2:5, Jesus told a paralyzed man, *"Son, thy sins be forgiven thee."* Some of the religious scholars who were there jumped all over those clear-cut words. They said, *"Why doth this man thus speak blasphemies? who can forgive sins but God only?"* (2:7).

The reply from Jesus, the Son of Man who came to offer His life as a sacrifice for all mankind, speaks volumes:

> *Why reason ye these things in your hearts? Whether is it easier to say to the sick of the palsy, Thy sins be forgiven thee; or to say, Arise, and take up thy bed, and walk? But that ye may know that the Son of man hath power on earth to forgive sins.* (Mark 2:8–10)

As an exclamation point that reaches through the centuries, Jesus immediately healed the paralyzed man (Mark 2:11–12)! The message was unmistakable to the people there, and it is unavoidable to us today. No one forgives sin but God. Sure, lots of people can say they are able to do amazing things, but only Jesus had the God-ordained authority to both heal and forgive sins. There was no confusion about what happened. Jesus clearly claimed and proved that He was the Son of God who was sent, not only in fulfillment of all prophecy, but was also here on earth to offer Himself as the substitute for all the sins of mankind.

The message was unmistakable to the people there, and it is unavoidable to us today. No one forgives sin but God.

What will you and I do with that same eternal challenge?

We cannot avoid looking into His eyes and making some sort of eternal decision. Faced with all the prophecies of the Bible and centuries of living proof that He indeed is *"the Lamb of God, which taketh away the sin of the world"* (John 1:29), we must accept Him as the eternal Savior.

C. S. Lewis, a famous Cambridge scholar and once-agnostic who decided to refute all the claims of the Bible and eventually became a Christian, pointed to the absurdity of the claims made by Jesus, had He not been truly the Savior sent from God:

> Among these Jews there suddenly turns up a man who goes about talking as if He was God. He claims to forgive sins. He says He has always existed. He says He is coming to judge the world at the end of time. Now let us get this clear. Among pantheists, like the Indians, anyone might say that he was a part of God, or one with God: there would be nothing very odd about it. But this man, since He was a Jew, could not mean that kind of God. God, in their language, meant the Being outside the world who had made it and was infinitely different from anything else. And when you have grasped that, you will see that what this man said was, quite simply, the most shocking thing that has ever been uttered by human lips.[2]

In other words, there was no middle ground. Writes Norman Anderson:

> He frequently made claims which would have sounded outrageous and blasphemous to Jewish ears, even from the lips of the greatest of prophets. He said that He was in existence before Abraham and that He was "lord" of the sabbath; He claimed to forgive sins; He frequently identified Himself (in His work, His person, and His glory) with the one He termed His heavenly Father; He accepted men's worship; and He said that He was to be the judge of men at the last day, when their eternal destiny

would depend on their attitude to Him. Then He died. It seems inescapable, therefore, that His resurrection must be interpreted as God's decisive vindication of these claims, while the alternative—the finality or the cross—would necessarily have implied the repudiation of His presumptuous and even blasphemous assertions.[3]

More to the point, C. S. Lewis, in his famous book *Mere Christianity*, makes this statement,

I am trying here to prevent anyone saying the really foolish thing that people often say about Him: "I'm ready to accept Jesus as a great moral teacher, but I don't accept His claim to be God." That is the one thing we must not say. A man who was merely a man and said the sort of things Jesus said would not be a great moral teacher. He would either be a lunatic—on a level with the man who says he is a poached egg—or else he would be the Devil of Hell. You must make your choice. Either this man was, and is, the son of God: or else a madman or something worse.[4]

Then Lewis strikes a deathblow into the heart of indecision concerning the Christ of Calvary:

You can shut Him up for a fool, you can spit at Him and kill Him as a demon; or you can fall at His feet and call Him Lord and God. But let us not come up with any patronizing non-sense about His being a great human teacher. He has not left that open to us. He did not intend to.[5]

When I made my decision to accept Jesus as Savior, it was without all the information I have given to you. What I have learned since the time I asked Christ Jesus into my heart as a teenager has only deepened my faith and increased my trust in His ability to direct my paths, now and throughout eternity. The depth of His love when He came to earth and offered Himself on Calvary is unexplainable. Who can truly understand it? All we must do is accept it.

That's why, from the beginning of time, our Father has given us so many examples of His eternal love being poured out upon each of us. One of the best, most understandable pictures comes from the Old Testament. With all the prophecies in mind that we discussed in this chapter, let's move quickly to a powerful illustration, given to His chosen people concerning the feasts of Israel and God's plan for our salvation. But before we move into the feasts, here are some additional prophecies and fulfillments of Christ's birth, life, ministry, death, and resurrection for your own study.

332 PROPHECIES FULFILLED

Prophecy	Given	Fulfilled
1. Seed of a woman (virgin birth)	Gen. 3:15	Luke 1:35; Matt. 1:18–20
2. He will bruise Satan's head	Gen. 3:15	Heb. 2:14; 1 John 3:18
3. Bodily ascension to heaven	Gen. 5:24	Mark 6:19
4. Son of Shem	Gen. 9:26–27	Luke 3:36
5. From Abraham's seed	Gen. 12:3	Acts 3:25–26
6. Promised to Abraham's seed	Gen. 12:7	Gal. 3:16
7. A priest after Melchizedek	Gen. 14:18	Heb. 6:20
8. A King also	Gen. 14:18	Heb. 7:2
9. Last Supper foreshadowed	Gen. 14:18	Matt. 26:26–29
10. Seed of Isaac	Gen. 17:19	Rom. 9:7
11. Lamb of God promised	Gen. 22:8	John 1:29
12. Isaac's seed will bless all nations	Gen. 22:18	Gal. 3:16
13. Redeemer from seed of Isaac	Gen. 26:2–5	Heb. 11:18
14. Time of His appearing	Gen. 49:10	Luke 2:1–7; Gal. 4:4
15. Seed of Judah	Gen. 49:10	Luke 3:33
16. Called Shiloh or "One Sent"	Gen. 49:10	John 17:3
17. Before Judah loses identity	Gen. 49:10	John 11:47–52
18. Obedience to Him	Gen. 49:10	John 10:16
19. The Great I AM	Exod. 3:13–14	John 4:26
20. A Lamb without blemish	Exod. 12:5	1 Pet. 1:19
21. Lamb's blood saves from wrath	Exod. 12:13	Rom. 5:8
22. Christ our Passover	Exod. 12:21–27	1 Cor. 5:7
23. No bone of the Lamb broken	Exod. 12:46	John 19:31–36
24. Exaltation predicted as Yeshua	Exod. 15:2	Acts 7:55–56
25. Holiness His character	Exod. 15:11	Luke 1:35; Acts 4:27
26. Spiritual Rock of Israel	Exod. 17:6	1 Cor. 10:4
27. Merciful	Exod. 33:19	Luke 1:72

Prophecy	Given	Fulfilled
28. Leper cleansed; priesthood sign	Lev. 14:11	Luke 5:12–14; Matt. 8:2
29. Christ's death once for all	Lev. 16:15–17	Heb. 9:7–14
30. Suffering outside the camp	Lev. 16:27	Matt. 27:33; Heb. 13:11–12
31. Blood, life of the flesh	Lev. 17:11	Matt. 26:28; Mark 10:45
32. Blood makes atonement	Lev. 17:11	John 3:14–18
33. "If any man thirst" drink offering	Lev. 23:36–37	John 19:31–36
34. Not a bone broken	Num. 9:12	John 19:31–36
35. Christ lifted up on cross	Num. 21:9	John 3:14–18
36. Time: "see him, but not now"	Num. 24:17	Gal. 4:4
37. A prophet would come	Deut. 18:15	John 6:14
38. Believed Moses, believe me	Deut. 18:15–16	John 5:45–47
39. Sent to speak Father's word	Deut. 18:18	John 8:28–29
40. Bear sin if you will not hear	Deut. 18:19	John 12:15
41. Cursed; hangs on a tree	Deut. 21:23	Gal. 3:10–13
42. Christ redeemed us	Ruth 4:4–9	Eph. 1:3–7
43. An anointed King to the Lord	1 Sam. 2:10	Matt. 28:18; John 12:15
44. David's seed	2 Sam. 7:12	Matt. 1:1
45. The Son of God	2 Sam. 7:14	Luke 1:32
46. Establish David's house forever	2 Sam. 7:16	Luke 3:31; Rev. 22:16
47. Bodily ascension to heaven	2 Kings 2:11	Luke 24:51
48. David's seed	1 Chron. 17:11	Matt. 1:1; 9:27
49. Reign on David's throne forever	1 Chron. 17:12–13	Luke 1:32–33
50. "I will be his Father, and he...my Son"	1 Chron. 17:13	Heb. 1:5
51. The Resurrection predicted	Job 19:23–27	John 5:24–29

Prophecy	Given	Fulfilled
52. Became lowly among men	Job 25:6	Matt. 27:30–31
53. Enmity of kings foreordained	Ps. 2:1–3	Acts 4:25–28
54. To own the title "Anointed"	Ps. 2:2	Acts 2:36
55. His character: holiness	Ps. 2:6	Rev. 3:7
56. To own the title King	Ps. 2:6	Matt. 2:2
57. Declared the Beloved Son	Ps. 2:7	Matt. 3:17
58. The Crucifixion and Resurrection	Ps. 2:7–8	Acts 13:29–33
59. Life comes through faith in Him	Ps. 2:12	John 20:31
60. Mouth of babes perfect His praise	Ps. 8:2	Matt. 21:16
61. His humiliation and exaltation	Ps. 8:5–6	Luke 24:50–53; 1 Cor. 15:27
62. Was not to see corruption	Ps. 16:10	Acts 2:31
63. Was to arise from the dead	Ps. 16:9–11	John 20:9
64. The Resurrection predicted	Ps. 17:15	Luke 24:6
65. Forsaken due to sins of others	Ps. 22:1	2 Cor. 5:21
66. Words from Calvary, "My God..."	Ps. 22:1	Mark 15:34
67. Darkness upon Calvary	Ps. 22:2	Matt. 27:45
68. They shake the head	Ps. 22:7	Matt. 27:39
69. Trusted God, let God help	Ps. 22:8	Matt. 27:43
70. Born the Savior	Ps. 22:9	Luke 2:7
71. Died of a broken heart	Ps. 22:14	John 19:34
72. Suffered agony on Calvary	Ps. 22:14–15	Mark 15:34–37
73. He thirsted	Ps. 22:15	John 19:28
74. Pierced His hands and feet	Ps. 22:16	John 19:34,37; 20:27
75. Stripped Him before men	Ps. 22:17–18	Luke 23:34–35
76. They parted His garments	Ps. 22:18	John 19:23–24
77. He committed Himself to God	Ps. 22:20–21	Luke 23:46
78. Satan bruised Redeemer's heel	Ps. 22:20–21	Heb. 2:14
79. His resurrection declared	Ps. 22:22	John 20:17
80. The Governor of the nations	Ps. 22:27–28	Col. 1:16

Prophecy	Given	Fulfilled
81. "It is finished"	Ps. 22:31	John 19:30
82. "I am the Good Shepherd"	Ps. 23:1	John 10:11
83. His exaltation predicted	Ps. 24:3	Acts 1:11; Phil. 2:9
84. His ascension	Ps. 24:7–10	John 7:33
85. His resurrection predicted	Ps. 30:3	Acts 2:32
86. "Into thy hands I commend my spirit"	Ps. 31:5	Luke 23:46
87. His acquaintances fled from Him	Ps. 31:11	Mark 14:50
88. Took counsel to put Him to death	Ps. 31:13	John 11:53
89. He trusted God, let Him deliver	Ps. 31:14–15	Matt. 27:43
90. Not a bone of Him broken	Ps. 34:20	John 19:31–36
91. False witnesses against Him	Ps. 35:11	Matt. 26:59
92. He was hated without a cause	Ps. 35:19	John 15:25
93. His friends stood afar off	Ps. 38:11	Luke 23:49
94. Joy of His resurrection predicted	Ps. 40:2–5	John 20:20
95. His delight, the will of the Father	Ps. 40:6–8	John 4:34
96. Righteousness preached in Israel	Ps. 40:9	Matt. 4:17
97. Confronted in the garden	Ps. 40:14	John 18:1
98. Betrayed by a familiar friend	Ps. 41:9	John 13:18
99. Grace came from His lips	Ps. 45:2	Luke 4:22
100. To own the title, God or Elohim	Ps. 45:6	Heb. 1:8
101. Anointed by the Holy Spirit	Ps. 45:7	Matt. 3:16; Heb.1:9
102. Called Christ (Messiah, Anointed)	Ps. 45:7–8	Luke 2:11
103. Worthy of our worship	Ps. 45:11	Matt. 2:2
104. Betrayed by a friend, not enemy	Ps. 55:12–14	John 13:18
105. Unrepentant death of betrayer	Ps. 55:15	Matt. 27:3–5; Acts 1:16–19
106. To give gifts to men	Ps. 68:18	Eph. 4:7–16
107. Ascended into heaven	Ps. 68:18	Luke 24:51
108. Hated without a cause	Ps. 69:4	John 15:25

Prophecy	Given	Fulfilled
109. A stranger to own brethren	Ps. 69:8	Luke 8:20–21
110. Zealous for the Lord's house	Ps. 69:9	John 2:17
111. Messiah's anguish before cross	Ps. 69:14–20	Matt. 26:36–45
112. "My soul is exceeding sorrowful"	Ps. 69:20	Matt. 26:38
113. Given vinegar in thirst	Ps. 69:21	Matt. 27:34
114. Savior given and smitten	Ps. 69:26	John 17:4; 18:11
115. Great persons were to visit Him	Ps. 72:10–11	Matt. 2:1–11
116. Corn of wheat fall to ground	Ps. 72:16	John 12:24
117. Name, Yinon, produce offspring	Ps. 72:17	John 1:12–13
118. All nations blessed by Him	Ps. 72:17	Acts 2:11–12,41
119. He would teach in parables	Ps. 78:1–2	Matt. 13:34–35
120. Spoke wisdom with authority	Ps. 78:2	Matt. 7:29
121. From the tribe of Judah	Ps. 78:67–68	Luke 3:33
122. He would have compassion	Ps. 86:15	Matt. 9:36
123. They stood afar off and watched	Ps. 88:8	Luke 23:49
124. Higher than earthly kings	Ps. 89:27	Luke 1:32–33
125. David's seed endures forever	Ps. 89:35–37	Luke 1:32–33
126. His character: faithfulness	Ps. 89:36–37	Rev. 1:5
127. He is from everlasting	Ps. 90:2; Mic. 5:2	John 1:1
128. Identified as messianic	Ps. 91:11–12	Luke 4:10–11
129. His exaltation predicted	Ps. 97:9	Acts 1:11; Eph. 1:20
130. His character: goodness	Ps. 100:5	Matt. 19:16–17
131. Suffering, reproach of Calvary	Ps. 102:1–11	John 19:16–18
132. Messiah is the preexistent Son	Ps. 102:25–27	Heb. 1:10–12
133. Ridiculed	Ps. 109:25	Matt. 27:39
134. Son of David	Ps. 110:1	Matt. 22:43
135. Ascend to right hand of Father	Ps. 110:1	Mark 16:19
136. David's son called Lord	Ps. 110:1	Matt. 22:44–45
137. Priest after Melchizedek's order	Ps. 110:4	Heb. 6:20
138. His character: compassionate	Ps. 112:4	Matt. 9:36

Prophecy	Given	Fulfilled
139. Resurrection assured	Ps. 118:17–18	Luke 24:5–7; 1 Cor. 15:20
140. Rejected stone is head of corner	Ps. 118:22–23	Matt. 21:42
141. Blessed One presented to Israel	Ps. 118:26	Matt. 21:9
142. To come while temple standing	Ps. 118:26	Matt. 21:12–15
143. Seed of David (fruit of His body)	Ps. 132:11	Luke 1:32
144. David's seed amazes kings	Ps. 138:1–6	Matt. 2:2–6
145. Earthly ministry of Christ	Ps. 147:3,6	Luke 4:18
146. He will send the Spirit of God	Ps. 147:18	John 16:7
147. A friend of sinners	Prov. 18:24	Matt. 11:19
148. The altogether lovely One	Song of Sol. 5:16	John 1:17
149. Judge among nations	Isa. 2:4	Luke 11:22
150. Beautiful branch and true vine	Isa. 4:2	John 15:1
151. When Isaiah saw His glory	Isa. 6:1	John 12:40–41
152. Parables fall on deaf ears	Isa. 6:9–10	Matt. 13:13–15
153. Blind to Christ, deaf to His words	Isa. 6:9–12	Acts 28:23–29
154. To be born of a virgin	Isa. 7:14	Luke 1:35
155. To be Emmanuel, God with us	Isa. 7:14	Matt. 1:18–23
156. Called Emmanuel	Isa. 8:8	Matt. 28:20
157. Stumbling stone, rock of offense	Isa. 8:14	1 Pet. 2:8
158. His ministry to begin in Galilee	Isa. 9:1–2	Matt. 4:12–17
159. A child born, humanity	Isa. 9:6	Luke 1:31
160. A Son given, deity	Isa. 9:6	Luke 1:32; John 1:14; 1 Tim. 3:16
161. Declared Son of God with power	Isa. 9:6	Rom. 1:3–4
162. The Wonderful One, Peleh	Isa. 9:6	Luke 4:22
163. The Counselor, Yaatz	Isa. 9:6	Matt. 13:54
164. The Mighty God, El Gibor	Isa. 9:6	Matt. 11:20
165. Everlasting Father, Avi Adth	Isa. 9:6	John 8:58
166. The Prince of Peace, Sar Shalom	Isa. 9:6	John 16:33
167. Establish everlasting kingdom	Isa. 9:7	Luke 1:32–33

Prophecy	Given	Fulfilled
168. His character: just	Isa. 9:7	John 5:30
169. No end government/throne/ peace	Isa. 9:7	Luke 1:32–33
170. Called a Nazarene	Isa. 11:1	Matt. 2:23
171. A rod out of Jesse, Son of Jesse	Isa. 11:1	Luke 3:23,32
172. The anointed One by the Spirit	Isa. 11:2	Matt. 3:16–17
173. His character: wisdom	Isa. 11:2	John 4:4–26
174. His character: truth	Isa. 11:4	John 14:6
175. The Gentiles seek Him	Isa. 11:10	John 12:18–21
176. Called Jesus, Yeshua (salvation)	Isa. 12:2	Matt. 1:21
177. The Resurrection predicted	Isa. 25:8	1 Cor. 15:54
178. Power of resurrection predicted	Isa. 26:19	John 11:43–44
179. Precious cornerstone	Isa. 28:16	Acts 4:11–12
180. Hypocritical obedience to Word	Isa. 29:13	Matt. 15:7–9
181. Wise confounded by the Word	Isa. 29:14	1 Cor. 1:18–31
182. A refuge, hiding place	Isa. 32:2	Matt. 23:37
183. He will come and save you	Isa. 35:4	Matt. 1:21
184. To have a ministry of miracles	Isa. 35:5	Matt. 11:4–6
185. Preceded by forerunner	Isa. 40:3–4	John 1:23
186. "Behold your God"	Isa. 40:9	John 1:36; 19:14
187. Shepherd, compassionate life-giver	Isa. 40:11	John 10:10–18
188. Faithful, patient redeemer	Isa. 42:1–4	Matt. 12:18–21
189. Meek and lowly	Isa. 42:2	Matt. 11:28–30
190. He brings hope for the hopeless	Isa. 42:3	John 4:1–26
191. Nations wait on His teachings	Isa. 42:4	John 12:20–26
192. The Light, salvation of Gentiles	Isa. 42:6	Luke 2:32
193. His is a worldwide compassion	Isa. 42:1,6	Matt. 28:19–20
194. Blind eyes opened	Isa. 42:7	John 9:25–38
195. He is the only Savior	Isa. 43:11	Acts 4:12
196. He will send the Spirit of God	Isa. 44:3	John 16:7,13
197. He will be the Judge	Isa. 45:23	John 5:22; Rom. 14:11

Prophecy	Given	Fulfilled
198. The first and the last	Isa. 48:12	John 1:30; Rev. 1:8,17
199. He came as Teacher	Isa. 48:17	John 3:2
200. Called from the womb	Isa. 49:1	Matt. 1:18
201. A Servant from the womb	Isa. 49:5	Luke 1:31; Phil. 2:7
202. He is salvation for Israel	Isa. 49:6	Luke 2:29–32
203. He is the Light of the Gentiles	Isa. 49:6	Acts 13:47
204. Salvation unto ends of the earth	Isa. 49:6	Acts 15:7–18
205. He is despised of the nation	Isa. 49:7	John 8:48–49
206. Heaven black at His humiliation	Isa. 50:3	Luke 23:44–45
207. Learned counselor for the weary	Isa. 50:4	Matt. 11:28–29
208. Servant bound willingly to obey	Isa. 50:5	Matt. 26:39
209. "I gave my back to the smiters"	Isa. 50:6	Matt. 27:26
210. He was smitten on the cheeks	Isa. 50:6	Matt. 26:67
211. He was spat upon	Isa. 50:6	Matt. 27:30
212. Publish good tidings of peace	Isa. 52:7	Luke 4:14–15
213. The Servant exalted	Isa. 52:13	Acts 1:8–11; Eph. 1:19–22
214. "Behold, my servant"	Isa. 52:13	Phil. 2:5–8
215. The Servant shockingly abused	Isa. 52:14	Luke 18:31–34; Matt. 26:67–68
216. Nations startled by His message	Isa. 52:15	Rom. 15:18–21
217. His blood shed, atonement for all	Isa. 52:15	Rev. 1:5
218. His people would not believe Him	Isa. 53:1	John 12:37–38
219. He grew up in a poor family	Isa. 53:2	Luke 2:7
220. Appearance of an ordinary man	Isa. 53:2	Phil. 2:7–8
221. Despised	Isa. 53:3	Luke 4:28–29
222. Rejected	Isa. 53:3	Matt. 27:21–23
223. Great sorrow and grief	Isa. 53:3	Luke 19:41–42
224. Men hide from His association	Isa. 53:3	Mark 14:50–52
225. He would have a healing ministry	Isa. 53:4	Luke 6:17–19
226. Bear the sins of the world	Isa. 53:4	1 Pet. 2:24
227. Thought to be cursed by God	Isa. 53:4	Matt. 27:41–43

Prophecy	Given	Fulfilled
228. Bears penalty for man's sin	Isa. 53:5	Luke 23:33
229. Peace between man and God	Isa. 53:5	Col. 1:20
230. His back would be whipped	Isa. 53:5	Matt. 27:26
231. Sin-Bearer for all mankind	Isa. 53:6	Gal. 1:4
232. God's will to bear man's sin	Isa. 53:6	1 John 4:10
233. Oppressed and afflicted	Isa. 53:7	Matt. 27:27–31
234. Silent before His accusers	Isa. 53:7	Matt. 27:12–14
235. Sacrificial Lamb	Isa. 53:7	John 1:29
236. Confined and persecuted	Isa. 53:8	Matt. 26:47—27:31
237. He would be judged	Isa. 53:8	John 18:13–22
238. Stricken and crucified	Isa. 53:8	Matt. 27:35
239. Dies for the sins of the world	Isa. 53:8	1 John 2:2
240. Buried in a rich man's grave	Isa. 53:9	Matt. 27:57
241. Innocent, had done no violence	Isa. 53:9	Mark 15:3
242. No deceit in his mouth	Isa. 53:9	John 18:38
243. God's will that He die for man	Isa. 53:10	John 18:11
244. An offering for sin	Isa. 53:10	Matt. 20:28
245. Resurrected and lives forever	Isa. 53:10	Mark 16:16
246. He would prosper	Isa. 53:10	John 17:1–5
247. God satisfied with His suffering	Isa. 53:11	John 12:27
248. God's servant	Isa. 53:11	Rom. 5:18–19
249. Would justify man before God	Isa. 53:11	Rom. 5:8–9
250. The Sin-Bearer for all mankind	Isa. 53:11	Heb. 9:28
251. Exalted by God for His sacrifice	Isa. 53:12	Matt. 28:18
252. Gave His life to save mankind	Isa. 53:12	Luke 23:46
253. Grouped with criminals	Isa. 53:12	Luke 23:32
254. Sin-Bearer for all mankind	Isa. 53:12	2 Cor. 5:21
255. Intercedes on man's behalf	Isa. 53:12	Luke 23:34
256. Resurrected by God	Isa. 55:3	Acts 13:34
257. A Witness	Isa. 55:4	John 18:37
258. Inhabits eternity, lives in heart	Isa. 57:15	Rom. 10:10
259. His ministry set captives free	Isa. 58:6	Luke 4:17–18

Prophecy	Given	Fulfilled
260. Came to provide salvation	Isa. 59:15–16	John 6:40
261. Intercedes between man and God	Isa. 59:15–16	Matt. 10:32
262. Came to Zion as Redeemer	Isa. 59:20	Luke 2:38
263. The Spirit of God upon Him	Isa. 61:1–2	Matt. 3:16–17
264. Preached the good news	Isa. 61:1–2	Luke 4:17–21
265. Provided freedom from bondage	Isa. 61:1–2	John 8:31–32
266. Proclaim a period of grace	Isa. 61:1–2	John 5:24
267. Power to save	Isa. 61:3	Matt. 9:6
268. Giving joy for mourning	Isa. 63:1	John 17:13
269. Descendant of David	Jer. 23:5–6	Luke 3:23–31
270. The Messiah would be God	Jer. 23:5–6	John 13:13
271. The Messiah both God and man	Jer. 23:5–6	1 Tim. 3:16
272. Born of a virgin	Jer. 31:22	Matt. 1:18–20
273. Messiah was the new covenant	Jer. 31:31	Matt. 26:28
274. Descendant of David	Jer. 33:14–15	Luke 3:23–31
275. Spoke words of God	Ezek. 2:1	John 17:8
276. Descendant of David	Ezek. 17:22–24	Luke 3:23–31
277. With amazement men marvel	Ezek. 32:10	Mark 5:20
278. Descendant of David	Ezek. 34:23–24	Matt. 1:1
279. He would ascend into heaven	Dan. 7:13–14	Acts 1:9–11
280. Highly exalted	Dan. 7:13–14	Eph. 1:20–22
281. His dominion everlasting	Dan. 7:13–14	Luke 1:31–33
282. To make an end to sins	Dan. 9:24	Gal. 1:3–5
283. He would be holy	Dan. 9:24	Luke 1:35
284. Decree to rebuild Jerusalem	Dan. 9:25	John 12:12–13
285. Messiah cut off	Dan. 9:26	Matt. 27:35
286. Die for the sins of the world	Dan. 9:26	Heb. 2:9
287. Killed before temple's destruction	Dan. 9:26	Matt. 27:50–51
288. Messiah in a glorified state	Dan. 10:5–6	Rev. 1:13–16
289. The personification of love	Hosea 11:4	2 Cor. 5:14
290. He would defeat death	Hosea 13:14	1 Cor. 15:55–57
291. His Spirit poured out	Joel 2:28	Acts 2:17–18

Prophecy	Given	Fulfilled
292. Offer salvation to all mankind	Joel 2:32	Rom. 10:12–13
293. Preexistence of Christ	Mic. 5:2	Heb. 1:8
294. Born in Bethlehem	Mic. 5:2	Matt. 2:1–2
295. God's servant	Mic. 5:2	John 15:10
296. From everlasting	Mic. 5:2	John 8:58
297. He would visit second temple	Hag. 2:6–9	Luke 2:27–32
298. Descendant of Zerubbabel	Hag. 2:23	Luke 3:23–27
299. God's servant	Zech. 3:8	John 17:4
300. Priest and King	Zech. 6:12–13	Heb. 8:1
301. Greeted with rejoicing in Jerusalem	Zech. 9:9	Matt. 21:8–10
302. Beheld as King	Zech. 9:9	John 12:12–13
303. The Messiah would be just	Zech. 9:9	John 5:30
304. The Messiah brought salvation	Zech. 9:9	Luke 19:10
305. The Messiah would be humble	Zech. 9:9	Matt. 11:29
306. Rode donkey into Jerusalem	Zech. 9:9	Matt. 21:6–9
307. The cornerstone	Zech. 10:4	Eph. 2:20
308. Unfit leaders in Israel	Zech. 11:4-6	Matt. 23:1–4
309. Protection removed at rejection	Zech. 11:4–6	Luke 19:41–44
310. Rejected in favor of another king	Zech. 11:4–6	John 19:13–15
311. Ministry to poor	Zech. 11:7	Matt. 9:35–36
312. Unbelief forces rejection	Zech. 11:8	Matt. 23:13–36
313. Despised and abhorred	Zech. 11:8	Matt. 27:20
314. Ceases ministry to His rejectors	Zech. 11:9	Matt. 3:10–11
315. Protection removed at rejection	Zech. 11:10–11	Luke 19:41–44
316. The Messiah would be God	Zech. 11:10–11	John 14:7
317. Betrayed for 30 pieces of silver	Zech. 11:12–13	Matt. 26:14–15
318. Rejected	Zech. 11:12–13	Matt. 26:14–15
319. Silver thrown into house of Lord	Zech. 11:12–13	Matt. 27:3–5
320. Messiah would be God	Zech. 11:12–13	John 12:45
321. Messiah's body would be pierced	Zech. 12:10	John 19:34–37
322. Messiah both God and man	Zech. 12:10	John 10:30

Prophecy	Given	Fulfilled
323. The Messiah would be rejected	Zech. 12:10	John 1:11
324. His will to die for mankind	Zech. 13:7	John 18:11
325. A violent death	Zech. 13:7	Matt. 27:35
326. Both God and man	Zech. 13:7	John 14:9
327. Israel scattered for rejecting Him	Zech. 13:7	Matt. 26:31–56
328. Messenger prepared the way	Mal. 3:1	Matt. 11:10
329. Sudden appearance at temple	Mal. 3:1	Mark 11:15–16
330. Messenger of the New Covenant	Mal. 3:1	Luke 4:43
331. Forerunner in the spirit of Elijah	Mal. 4:5	Matt. 3:1–2
332. Turn many to righteousness	Mal. 4:6	Luke 1:16–17

2

FROM THE PASSOVER TO THE CROSS: 21 REMARKABLE REVELATIONS

And beginning at Moses and all the prophets, he expounded unto them in all the scriptures the things concerning himself.

—LUKE 24:27

ING SOLOMON, a name synonymous with wisdom, once wrote, *"It is the glory of God to conceal a thing: but the honour of kings is to search out a matter"* (Proverbs 25:2).

God's glory is concealed through His Word, but the believer, as a kingly priest, can see His glory revealed by careful searching. God's Word is a treasure to be discovered. The deep truths cannot always be mined by merely scratching on the surface.

When you study the Bible with an open mind, it's truly an amazing adventure to see all God has provided. Everywhere, it seems, the Father has given guideposts which point toward the ultimate treasure, His Son, Jesus Christ. To mine these eternal riches, even as with earthly jewels or precious ore, you are required to dig beneath the surface. That's why it is so important to ask the Father to give supernatural wisdom as you search the Word for fresh, priceless, life-giving resources every day.

OLD TESTAMENT TREASURES

I'm convinced that it is impossible to fully understand the New Testament truths without a thorough understanding of the Old Testament. All the foundations for the final twenty-seven books of the Bible are laid in the first thirty-nine books. The New Testament is the fulfillment of the Old. Each is incomplete without the other.

The New in the Old is concealed; the Old in the New is revealed!

The New in the Old is concealed; the Old in the New is revealed! Praise God for the fact that we have both.

And one of the most remarkable treasures in all of Scripture is the study of the feasts which God outlined through the instructions He gave to the children of Israel:

Moses' Teachings with their yearly cycle of sacrifices are only a shadow of the good things in the future. They aren't an exact likeness of those things. They can never make those who worship perfect. If these sacrifices could have made the worshipers perfect, the sacrifices would have stopped long ago. Those who worship would have been cleansed once and for all. Their consciences would have been free from sin. Instead, this yearly cycle of sacrifices reminded people of their sins. (The blood of bulls and goats cannot take away sins.) For this reason, when Christ came into the world, he said, "You did not want sacrifices and offerings, but you prepared a body for me. You did not approve of burnt offerings and sacrifices for sin.

Then I said, 'I have come! (It is written about me in the scroll of the book.) I have come to do what you want, my God.'" In this passage Christ first said, "You did not want sacrifices, offerings, burnt offerings, and sacrifices for sin. You did not approve of them." (These are the sacrifices that Moses' Teachings require people to offer.) Then Christ says, "I have come to do what you want." He did away with sacrifices in order to establish the obedience that God wants. We have been set apart as holy because Jesus Christ did what God wanted him to do by sacrificing his body once and for all. (Hebrews 10:1–10, GW)

Jesus offered Himself as a sacrifice for our sins, "once and for all," so we don't have to live under the curse of the law. Jesus came to fulfill the Old Covenant, not to destroy it. And as I've mentioned already, you cannot fully understand the New Testament until you grasp the meaning of the Old Testament. It is impossible! Neither can you truly comprehend the depths of all that Jesus did for us on the cross until you peer closely into the meaning of the feasts of Israel.

Therefore, I believe there are many motivations for studying the feasts of Israel. Here are seven important reasons which have helped me immeasurably in my own walk with the Lord:

1. The feasts reveal Christ Jesus, through and through.
2. The feasts offer present truth, which the Holy Spirit uses to quicken us.
3. The feasts help us to learn how to hear the voice of the Holy Spirit. In them, we hear God's voice. There are treasures in the feasts that have been sadly ignored and neglected.
4. The feasts are a shadow of things to come. You can understand prophecy better and be prepared for what is to come.
5. The feasts are filled with prophetic types, symbols, and examples. They are examples and patterns for us to follow Christ with greater wisdom.
6. The feasts offer a wealth of information for us. Upon these truths we can build our lives. We learn much about life, especially fellowship with the Father and His Son, Jesus Christ.

We learn more about honoring and following the guidance of the Holy Spirit.

7. The feasts reveal heavenly things, giving us an eternal hope.

Sadly, some people excuse studying the feasts of Israel and the Old Covenant by saying, "I just don't understand all the symbolism and the ways they did it back then. Besides, we're under grace, not under law." Jesus made it very clear that He came to fulfill the law, not destroy it. It's time we must study these vital lessons taught first to the children of Israel. Without them, we get an incomplete picture of what Christ Jesus did on the cross.

Since you were a child you've undoubtedly heard the phrase, "A picture is worth a thousand words." This is certainly true with the feasts of Israel. They are graphic object lessons. From the time they were given to the children of Israel, these laws were ever-present visual aids, or pictures, if you will, to use physical rituals to help them understand spiritual truth and to walk therein.

THREE FEAST SEASONS, SEVEN FEASTS

As recorded in Leviticus 23, God instructed the children of Israel to hold three feast seasons, observing seven holy gatherings each year, and established them on the Jewish calendar so the people would need to travel to Jerusalem three times a year.

> And the LORD spake unto Moses, saying, Speak unto the children of Israel, and say unto them, Concerning the feasts of the LORD, which ye shall proclaim to be holy convocations, even these are my feasts. Six days shall work be done: but the seventh day is the sabbath of rest, a holy convocation; ye shall do no work therein: it is the sabbath of the LORD in all your dwellings. These are the feasts of

the LORD, *even holy convocations, which ye shall proclaim in their seasons.* (Leviticus 23:1–4)

These three feast seasons were called Passover, Pentecost, and Tabernacles, which represented the three major links between God and His covenant children. Just as there are three major colors in the rainbow, and these three are manifest in seven shades, so it is with the feasts. There are three major feast seasons, and these feasts are broken up into seven specific feasts. And each of the seven feasts hold a wealth of information which can illuminate our understanding of Jesus Christ and all He has done for each of us.

Let me give a quick overview of each. Then I'll continue in more detail about each specific feast and the fulfillment of each in chapter 3.

PASSOVER SEASON: FEASTS OF PASSOVER, UNLEAVENED BREAD, AND FIRSTFRUITS

The purpose of this first season has always been to teach the children of Israel how to find and enter God's true peace. This season took place in the first month of the Jewish year.

The first feast was outlined in Leviticus 23:5: *"In the fourteenth day of the first month at even is the* LORD'*s passover."* The second feast was given in Leviticus 23:6-8:

> *And on the fifteenth day of the same month is the feast of unleavened bread unto the* LORD: *seven days ye must eat unleavened bread. In the first day ye shall have an holy convocation: ye shall do no servile work therein. But ye shall offer an offering made by fire unto the* LORD *seven days: in the seventh day is a holy convocation: ye shall do no servile work therein.*

The third and final feast of the Passover season is spoken of or known as the day of the sheaf of the firstfruits of harvest.

> *And the LORD spake unto Moses, saying, Speak unto the children of Israel, and say unto them, When ye be come into the land which I give unto you, and shall reap the harvest thereof, then ye shall bring a sheaf of the firstfruits of your harvest unto the priest: And he shall wave the sheaf before the LORD, to be accepted for you: on the morrow after the sabbath the priest shall wave it. And ye shall offer that day when ye wave the sheaf an he lamb without blemish of the first year for a burnt offering unto the LORD. And the meat offering thereof shall be two tenth deals of fine flour mingled with oil, an offering made by fire unto the LORD for a sweet savour: and the drink offering thereof shall be of wine, the fourth part of a hin. And ye shall eat neither bread, nor parched corn, nor green ears, until the selfsame day that ye have brought an offering unto your God: it shall be a statute for ever throughout your generations in all your dwellings.* (Leviticus 23:9–14)

PENTECOST SEASON: A SINGLE GATHERING

This feast took place during the third month of the Jewish calendar. After crossing the Red Sea and being led by the pillar of fire, the children of Israel were brought to the foot of Mount Sinai, where they experienced the Feast of Pentecost and the receiving of the Law.

> *And ye shall count unto you from the morrow after the sabbath, from the day that ye brought the sheaf of the wave offering; seven sabbaths shall be complete: Even unto the morrow after the seventh sabbath shall ye number fifty days; and ye shall offer a new meat*

offering unto the LORD. Ye shall bring out of your habitations two wave loaves of two tenth deals: they shall be of fine flour; they shall be baken with leaven; they are the first fruits unto the LORD. And ye shall offer with the bread seven lambs without blemish of the first year, and one young bullock, and two rams: they shall be for a burnt offering unto the LORD, with their meat offering, and their drink offerings, even an offering made by fire, of sweet savour unto the LORD. Then ye shall sacrifice one kid of the goats for a sin offering, and two lambs of the first year for a sacrifice of peace offerings. And the priest shall wave them with the bread of the first fruits for a wave offering before the LORD, with the two lambs: they shall be holy to the LORD for the priest. And ye shall proclaim on the self-same day, that it may be a holy convocation unto you: ye shall do no servile work therein: it shall be a statute for ever in all your dwellings throughout your generations. And when ye reap the harvest of your land, thou shalt not make clean riddance of the corners of thy field when thou reapest, neither shalt thou gather any gleaning of thy harvest: thou shalt leave them unto the poor, and to the stranger: I am the LORD your God. (Leviticus 23:15–22)

TABERNACLES SEASON: THE FEAST OF TRUMPETS, DAY OF ATONEMENT, AND FEAST OF TABERNACLES

This third season of feasts was instituted during the seventh month of the Jewish calendar. The purpose of this season was to teach the children of Israel how to enter God's rest and protection.

The Feast of Trumpets is given in Leviticus 23:23–25:

And the LORD spake unto Moses, saying, Speak unto the children of Israel, saying, In the seventh month, in the first day of the month, shall ye have a sabbath, a memorial of blowing of trumpets, an holy convocation. Ye shall do no servile work therein: but ye shall offer an offering made by fire unto the LORD.

The Day of Atonement was detailed in Leviticus 23:26–32:

And the LORD spake unto Moses, saying, Also on the tenth day of this seventh month there shall be a day of atonement: it shall be an holy convocation unto you; and ye shall afflict your souls, and offer an offering made by fire unto the LORD. And ye shall do no work in that same day: for it is a day of atonement, to make an atonement for you before the LORD your God. For whatsoever soul it be that shall not be afflicted in that same day, he shall be cut off from among his people. And whatsoever soul it be that doeth any work in that same day, the same soul will I destroy from among his people. Ye shall do no manner of work: it shall be a statute for ever throughout your generations in all your dwellings. It shall be unto you a sabbath of rest, and ye shall afflict your souls: in the ninth day of the month at even, from even unto even, shall ye celebrate your sabbath.

The Feast of Tabernacles is given in Leviticus 23:33–44:

And the LORD spake unto Moses, saying, Speak unto the children of Israel, saying, The fifteenth day of this seventh month shall be the feast of tabernacles for seven days unto the LORD. On the first day shall be a holy convocation: ye shall do no servile work therein. Seven days ye shall offer an offering made by fire unto the LORD: on the eighth day shall be a holy convocation unto you; and ye shall offer an offering made by fire unto the LORD: it is a solemn assembly; and ye shall do no servile work therein. These are the feasts of the LORD, which ye shall proclaim to be holy convoca-

tions, to offer an offering made by fire unto the LORD, a burnt offering, and a meat offering, a sacrifice, and drink offerings, every thing upon his day: Beside the sabbaths of the LORD, and beside your gifts, and beside all your vows, and beside all your freewill offerings, which ye give unto the LORD. Also in the fifteenth day of the seventh month, when ye have gathered in the fruit of the land, ye shall keep a feast unto the LORD seven days: on the first day shall be a sabbath, and on the eighth day shall be a sabbath. And ye shall take you on the first day the boughs of goodly trees, branches of palm trees, and the boughs of thick trees, and willows of the brook; and ye shall rejoice before the LORD your God seven days. And ye shall keep it a feast unto the LORD seven days in the year. It shall be a statute for ever in your generations: ye shall celebrate it in the seventh month. Ye shall dwell in booths seven days; all that are Israelites born shall dwell in booths: That your generations may know that I made the children of Israel to dwell in booths, when I brought them out of the land of Egypt: I am the LORD your God. And Moses declared unto the children of Israel the feasts of the LORD.

Each of these feasts was (and continues to be) extremely significant times for the Hebrews, for these feasts taught the children of Israel and their descendents to honor God for what He had done in their lives. More importantly, each feast pointed to the Messiah, distinctively describing a vital part of His life and ministry.

In Israel, the feasts were observed. In Christ, the feasts were fulfilled. In the church, the feasts are applied. We must learn to apply each, and we must apply them in order to have victory every day.

During the Passover season, in the Feast of the Passover, the Lamb died so we might receive salvation. In the Feast of Unleavened Bread, we received deliverance from sin, so we must turn from our disobedience. In the Feast of Firstfruits, we rise to newness of life, a brand-new creation, leaving the old things behind.

During the single feast of the Pentecost season, we are endued with the power of the Holy Ghost, which is exactly what happened in Acts 2:1–4, as Christ's followers sought the Lord's power and direction during this season:

> *And when the day of Pentecost was fully come, they were all with one accord in one place. And suddenly there came a sound from heaven as of a rushing mighty wind, and it filled all the house where they were sitting. And there appeared unto them cloven tongues like as of fire, and it sat upon each of them. And they were all filled with the Holy Ghost, and began to speak with other tongues, as the Spirit gave them utterance.*

During the Tabernacles season, in the Feast of Trumpets, the gathering of Israel points to the rapture of the saints of God. During the Day of Atonement, Israel was cleansed, pointing to the sanctification of the church and the national cleansing of God's chosen people. And during the Feast of Tabernacles, the main themes are fruit, harvest, and latter rain, pointing to the ultimate reign of Christ.

As with the prophecies discussed in chapter 1 of this book, these feasts were given specifically to point the nation of Israel toward the time when the Messiah would come to earth.

It is interesting to note that eight times in Leviticus, as God outlined the seven feasts, He told Israel that they were to do no work during these special times. So it is with us today. To be able to understand who we are in Christ, we must cease from the work of the flesh:

> *Now the works of the flesh are manifest, which are these; adultery, fornication, uncleanness, lasciviousness, idolatry, witchcraft, hatred,*

variance, emulations, wrath, strife, seditions, heresies, envyings, murders, drunkenness, revellings, and such like: of the which I tell you before, as I have also told you in time past, that they which do such things shall not inherit the kingdom of God. (Galatians 5:19–21)

According to Romans 3:27–28, we must stop focusing on the works of the law: *"Where is boasting then? It is excluded. By what law? of works? Nay: but by the law of faith. Therefore we conclude that a man is justified by faith without the deeds of the law."* We must cease from the works of the law and find rest in Jesus. Remember in Matthew 11:27–30, the Savior called us to rest in Him so we could know Him better:

All things are delivered unto me of my Father: and no man knoweth the Son, but the Father: neither knoweth any man the Father, save the Son, and he to whomsoever the Son will reveal him. Come unto me, all ye that labor and are heavy laden, and I will give you rest. Take my yoke upon you, and learn of me; for I am meek and lowly in heart: and ye shall find rest unto your souls. For my yoke is easy, and my burden is light.

The Master told His followers, *"Think not that I am come to destroy the law, or the prophets: I am not come to destroy, but to fulfil"* (Matthew 5:17). The shadows contained in the feasts of Israel reveal timeless truths, given to help us honor God today for all He has done in our lives, just as the children of Israel were taught. Even more importantly, the feasts provide an in-depth look into the Savior's life and ministry, as well as pointing to all that He did to redeem us from sin.

The feasts deal with the rest we receive in Christ Jesus. It is rest. If you are not resting, you cannot be feasting. Only those who know how to rest can experience Passover, Unleavened Bread, Firstfruit, Pentecost, Trumpets, Atonement, and Tabernacles.

The Passover Victory

Let's focus on the Passover Feast. In chapter 3, I'll discuss more deeply the other six feasts of Israel.

As you understand the Passover, your foundation will be strengthened. When the storms of life come at you in the future, you will not be shaken. In this feast is your deliverance from sin and sickness. Sadly, some believers have not yet applied what God has provided through this feast. As long as sickness is still in the body, Passover has not been fully applied. Yet I believe we are coming into it. We're about to see Passover fulfilled completely. We're coming out of Egypt all the way!

According to the book of Exodus, Moses, who was raised in Pharaoh's household, had fled the country after slaying an Egyptian, then spent forty years tending flocks in the desert. While there, he was met by God and instructed to go to Pharaoh and demand the freedom of his people.

You remember how the pharaoh ignored Moses and the repeated requests for freedom. As a result, God unleashed a series of ten horrible plagues upon the nation of Egypt (Exodus 7-11): blood, frogs, lice, flies, death of livestock, boils, hail, locusts, darkness, and slaying of the firstborn.

When the final plague was announced, God declared, "*About midnight will I go out into the midst of Egypt: And all the firstborn in the land of Egypt shall die*" (Exodus 11:4–5).

At the same time, the Lord told Moses He was about to give His people a new beginning:

> And the LORD spake unto Moses and Aaron in the land of Egypt, saying, This month shall be unto you the beginning of months: it shall be the first month of the year to you. Speak ye unto all the congregation of Israel, saying, In the tenth day of this month they shall take to them every man a lamb, according to the house of their

fathers, a lamb for a house: And if the household be too little for the lamb, let him and his neighbor next unto his house take it according to the number of the souls; every man according to his eating shall make your count for the lamb. Your lamb shall be without blemish, a male of the first year: ye shall take it out from the sheep, or from the goats: And ye shall keep it up until the fourteenth day of the same month: and the whole assembly of the congregation of Israel shall kill it in the evening. And they shall take of the blood, and strike it on the two side posts and on the upper door post of the houses, wherein they shall eat it. And they shall eat the flesh in that night, roast with fire, and unleavened bread; and with bitter herbs they shall eat it. Eat not of it raw, nor sodden at all with water, but roast with fire; his head with his legs, and with the purtenance thereof. And ye shall let nothing of it remain until the morning; and that which remaineth of it until the morning ye shall burn with fire. And thus shall ye eat it; with your loins girded, your shoes on your feet, and your staff in your hand; and ye shall eat it in haste: it is the LORD's passover. For I will pass through the land of Egypt this night, and will smite all the firstborn in the land of Egypt, both man and beast; and against all the gods of Egypt I will execute judgment: I am the LORD. And the blood shall be to you for a token upon the houses where ye are: and when I see the blood, I will pass over you, and the plague shall not be upon you to destroy you, when I smite the land of Egypt. And this day shall be unto you for a memorial; and ye shall keep it a feast to the LORD throughout your generations. (Exodus 12:1–14)

Notice that the children of Israel were instructed to keep the lamb until the fourteenth day of the month and to kill it in the evening (verse 6). Before eating, they were to *"take of the blood, and strike it on the two side posts and on the upper door post of the houses"* (verse 7). God told them to eat all of the lamb, for *"it is the Lord's passover"* (verse 11).

Why was the shedding of blood, eating the lamb, and the application of blood on the two sideposts and on the upper door posts of the houses so important? I will explain the answer to that question throughout the remainder of this chapter. The simple answer is that, on the last night, God said He would pass through the land and smite the firstborn in the land of Egypt (verse 12). The lamb's shed blood became their salvation.

Passover, or the Hebrew word *pesach* literally means passing over, protection and deliverance, and it comes from the explicit instructions given by God to Moses on the night the angel of death passed over those homes marked with blood. The Passover Feast celebrates this miraculous history.

THE TWENTY-ONE REVELATIONS OF THE CROSS

When God gave the instruction to Moses, and when Moses, in turn, repeated these directions to the children of Israel, the gospel of Jesus Christ was preached. The blood on the door posts and side posts brought safety and so much more. So, it is no mere coincidence that these Holy Spirit–inspired words were given in 1 Corinthians 5:7: *"For even Christ our passover is sacrificed for us."* He is your Passover! He is your *Pesach*, your Protection, your Deliverer!

What He did on the cross was the fulfillment of the Word given to Moses and the children of Israel. As we study the Feast of Passover, it is vital that we understand what truly happened on the cross through these twenty-one revelations.

1. The Cross begins our life.

Exodus 12:1–2 explains: *"And the LORD spake unto Moses and Aaron in the land of Egypt, saying, This month shall be unto you the beginning of months: it shall be the first month of the year to you."* As God gave directions for the Passover Feast, He also foretold another coming date change.

The Cross always starts a new beginning. The Cross always changes the calendar. The Cross erases the past. Because of the Cross

he Cross always starts a new beginning.

"if any man be in Christ, he is a new creature: old things are passed away; behold, all things are become new" (2 Corinthians 5:17). The first revelation of the Cross is enough to set you free! Some still struggle with this. They have not understood. They still condemn themselves for the sins of yesterday, but *"there is therefore now no condemnation to them which are in Christ Jesus, who walk not after the flesh, but after the Spirit"* (Romans 8:1).

We must not insult God. The Cross erased your yesterday, for it changed your calendar forever. Certainly what Jesus did on the cross changed mankind's date system, but the Word makes it clear that Christ went to the cross to make a change in each believer's life, as well.

Your calendar has changed! You are no longer your own; you belong to Jesus. You once belonged to the devil, but now you belong to Jesus, the Prince of Life. That's why Satan hates the work of the Cross and the new birth that is made possible through what happened at Calvary. That's why he keeps bringing up your past. That's why the enemy of our soul throws everything we've ever done back at us. There is no past with God. And if the devil reminds you of your yesterday, remind him of his tomorrow!

With the new birth through *"the Lamb of God which taketh away the sin of the world"* (John 1:29), as with Passover, the calender changed. It's a new day of freedom and deliverance. Old things are gone, forgotten, and erased. When you accept the work of Calvary, you become a new creation! It's a new life. It will be the beginning of months to you. Now it is up to you to live it.

2. The Passover Lamb was ordained to die in due time.

During the Passover Feast, Israel was given very specific instructions:

> *Speak ye unto all the congregation of Israel, saying, In the tenth day of this month they shall take to them every man a lamb, according to the house of their fathers, a lamb for an house: And if the household be too little for the lamb, let him and his neighbor next unto his house take it according to the number of the souls; every man according to his eating shall make your count for the lamb. Your lamb shall be without blemish, a male of the first year: ye shall take it out from the sheep, or from the goats: And ye shall keep it up until the fourteenth day of the same month: and the whole assembly of the congregation of Israel shall kill it in the evening.* (Exodus 12:3–6)

God said to the children of Israel to take the lamb on the tenth day and set it aside until the fourteenth day. God told the Jewish nation not to touch or kill the passover lamb until the fourteenth day. It was an exact time of preparation for death. This was fulfilled in Christ Jesus completely.

It's no mere coincidence that the Lamb of God entered Jerusalem on the tenth day of the month and was slain on the fourteenth day! That's a historic fact, confirmed by Scripture.

It's also no coincidence that the time from the first Adam to the second Adam, the Lamb of God, was four thousand years of preparation. That's four days, according to 2 Peter 3:8: "But, beloved, be not ignorant of this one thing, that one day is with the Lord as a thousand years, and a thousand years as one day."

The psalmist points to this truth, as well, in Psalm 90:4: "*For a thousand years in thy sight are but as yesterday when it is past, and as a watch in the night.*"

What a glorious revelation! The time frame from Adam to Christ was four thousand years. Because God is not confined by time and is not surprised by anything, and because He is omniscient, He knew that man would need a Savior. He ordained that His Son would be the Lamb of God to be slain for the sins of mankind. Jesus was set aside for four thousand years, just as God told Moses to make sure the children of Israel set aside the Passover lamb four days.

The Scripture goes on to say this about the Lamb's anointed time to die:

> *Forasmuch as ye know that ye were not redeemed with corruptible things, as silver and gold, from your vain conversation received by tradition from your fathers; but with the precious blood of Christ, as of a lamb without blemish and without spot: Who verily was foreordained before the foundation of the world, but was manifest in these last times for you.* (1 Peter 1:18–20)

Not only was the Lord Jesus set aside four thousand years, but He walked into Jerusalem in fulfillment of Exodus 12:3–6, which we read earlier. So accurate is prophecy that Jesus entered Jerusalem on the tenth day of the first month, arriving on what we now call Palm Sunday. As He entered the city, He was welcomed by throngs of people who cried out, "Hosanna! King of kings!" Following His triumphant entry into Jerusalem, one day passed. Two days passed. Three days passed. On the fourth, which had to be Wednesday, not Friday as some people think, He went to the cross. He did not die on Friday. This is supported in the feasts of Israel, because every Jewish Passover season observes two sabbaths. High Sabbath was (and still is) observed on the day we call Wednesday. The regular Sabbath was (and still is) observed on the day we call Saturday.

Jesus died on the High Sabbath. Remember, He entered Jerusalem on Sunday, or the first day of the week. He was in Jerusalem four days before He was crucified. That was on Wednesday, on the High Sabbath of Passover, which was also the fourteenth day of the first month on the Jewish calendar.

Here was the Messiah, fulfilling the most detailed of prophecies, yet the children of Israel could not see it. They could not understand when they saw Him enter the Old City, palm branches waving and people crying, "Hosanna to the King." They certainly could not see it four days later when He went to the cross.

Two thousand years later we have the advantage of hindsight. We can look at Scripture and see how remarkably the Lamb of God fulfilled prophecy and in such detail. This should strengthen our faith if we are willing to dig below the surface and focus on the eternal treasures beneath.

We live in a time when the world's answers are falling short, when the foundations are being shaken. Oh, that God would raise up an army of believers around the world who will stand on the firm foundation of faith to deliver the saving and miracle-working gospel of Jesus Christ.

I pray that these revelations of the Lamb of God will help you win multitudes of people to the Lord in the coming days. May your harvest of souls be greater than you ever imagined! May you win men and women who have mocked you for your faith. I'm confident that you will reach people who have said, "We don't want anything to do with God." I write these words in faith because I believe you are going to be a voice of certainty in an age of increasing uncertainty. Christ has fulfilled every prophecy, and you can point people to Christ our Passover Lamb with absolute confidence.

3. Christ was the Lamb of God without blemish.

God instructed the children of Israel concerning the purity of the lamb which would be sacrificed at Passover: *"Your lamb shall be without blemish, a male of the first year: ye shall take it out from the sheep, or from the goats"* (Exodus 12:5).

There could be no spot or blemish. Nothing! The inspection process, from the very first Passover, was extremely thorough to guarantee a lamb that met the strictest standards set by God.

The Lamb of God, without question, fulfilled every criteria. The Lamb of God is perfect. He is without blemish. He is holy, righteous, and just: *"For as much as ye know that ye were not redeemed with corruptible things, as silver and gold, from your vain conversation received by tradition from your fathers; but with the precious blood of Christ, as of a lamb without blemish and without spot* (1 Peter 1:18–19). In fact, if you look closely through the Scriptures, you will see that before He cried, *"My God, my God, why hast thou forsaken me?"* (Mark 15:34), Christ Jesus actually went through seven distinct inspections:

• **Pilate** inspected Jesus, and in John 19:4 we read, *"Pilate therefore went forth again, and saith unto them, Behold, I bring him forth to you, that ye may know that I find no fault in him."* No fault!

• **King Herod** inspected the Savior. Jesus, by King Herod's own admission of Christ's blamelessness, did nothing worthy of death. Luke 23:13–15 details Pilate's account of the obvious result of the king's scrutiny:

> *And Pilate, when he had called together the chief priests and the rulers and the people, Said unto them, Ye have brought this man unto me, as one that perverteth the people: and, behold, I, having examined him before you, have found no fault in this man touching*

those things whereof ye accuse him: No, nor yet Herod: for I sent
you to him; and, lo, nothing worthy of death is done unto him.

• **Annas,** father-in-law of the high priest, inspected Jesus. Annas obviously found no fault, for he passed Him along to his son-in-law. The examination is found in John 18:12–14, 24:

> *Then the band and the captain and officers of the Jews took Jesus,*
> *and bound him, And led him away to Annas first; for he was father*
> *in law to Caiaphas, which was the high priest that same year. Now*
> *Caiaphas was he, which gave counsel to the Jews, that it was expe-*
> *dient that one man should die for the people.... Now Annas had*
> *sent him bound unto Caiaphas the high priest.*

• **Caiaphas,** the high priest, inspected Jesus, as reflected in John 18. Again, no blame could be placed on the spotless Lamb of God.

• **Judas** inspected the Savior. He spent nearly three years with the Son of God and betrayed the Savior for thirty pieces of silver. He mourned that action later by trying to undo his treachery. Flinging the money on the floor, the traitor of all traitors cried, *"I have sinned in that I have betrayed the innocent blood"* (Matthew 27:4).

• **The centurion** inspected the Master. The commander of the Roman soldiers, when it was finished, gave the awe-filled result of his crucifixion scrutiny: *"Now when the centurion, and they that were with him, watching Jesus, saw the earthquake, and those things that were done, they feared greatly, saying, Truly this was the Son of God"* (Matthew 27:54). Matthew Henry, the noted Bible scholar, writes of the centurion's excla-mation, "The best of his disciples could not have said more at any time, and at this time they had not faith and courage enough to say thus much."

• **The thief** hanging beside Jesus inspected the Lamb of God closely during Christ's final hours on the cross, and this common criminal made a powerful confession that propelled him into an eternity with the Savior:

> *But the other answering rebuked him, saying, Dost not thou fear God, seeing thou art in the same condemnation? And we indeed justly; for we receive the due reward of our deeds: but this man hath done nothing amiss. And he said unto Jesus, Lord, remember me when thou comest into thy kingdom.* (Luke 23:40–42)

Seven inspections came and went. Seven confessions pointed to the irrefutable fact that no one could find fault in Him. As proclaimed truthfully by the thief, the fault is in each of us. We are to blame.

Oh, thank God that seven, as with the inspections and confessions, is also the biblical number of salvation. Since He was (and is) blameless, without spot or blemish, the Lamb of God can seek and save a lost world full of blame-filled, spotted, and blemished lost sheep. We can be saved through the blameless One, "*For he hath made him to be sin for us, who knew no sin; that we might be made the righteousness of God in him*" (2 Corinthians 5:21).

4. Christ, the firstborn Lamb, was actually the second born.

I referred to Exodus 12:5 in the previous revelations. Let me return again: "*Your lamb shall be without blemish, a male of the first year: ye shall take it out from the sheep, or from the goats.*" First year refers to firstborn. The inheritance, in Scripture and throughout most cultures, belongs primarily or solely to the firstborn male.

Jesus was the firstborn of Mary, yet it's important to notice that every description of the Messiah given in the Bible referred to the second man, not the first man, the second born, not the firstborn. This theme, when you look into the Scriptures, shows how Adam was set aside for the second Adam, Jesus Christ. Cain was set aside for Abel. Ishmael was set aside for Isaac. Esau was set aside for Jacob. In each instance, the firstborn was of the flesh; the second was made the first-born through the spirit. Only the spiritual order of birth matters.

What God means by firstborn is not what humans mean. Firstborn is not what we as human beings understand, for we see only in the flesh; however, God only sees what is of the Spirit. To us, we are born. To Him, we are born again. To you, no matter when you were born, you can be firstborn in the Spirit.

That is what happened to me. I was the second child born to my parents, but I was the first member of the family to accept Jesus Christ as my Savior. Eventually all of my family came to Christ, and each could claim the inheritance of Christ, no matter the order in which they became believers. Your parents may see you as number two or five or seven in the flesh, yet because of the work of Calvary, the Holy Spirit sees you as firstborn in the spirit. Regardless of your natural birth order, because of the Cross you can participate in the Lamb of God's inheritance. To you belongs the inheritance and the promises.

5. Righteousness came through one, the Man called Christ Jesus.

The prophecies and revelations about the Cross were fulfilled in the most intimate detail. Again in Exodus 12:5, there is no doubt that the Passover lamb should be a male: *"Your lamb shall be without blemish, a male of the first year: ye shall take it out from the sheep, or from the goats."*

Romans 5:12 points to the fulfillment on the cross: *"Wherefore, as by one man sin entered into the world, and death by sin; and so death passed upon all men, for that all have sinned."*

Romans 5:17–19 echoes that wonderful fulfillment:

For if by one man's offence death reigned by one; much more they which receive abundance of grace and of the gift of righteousness shall reign in life by one, Jesus Christ. Therefore as by the offence of one judgment came upon all men to condemnation; even so by the righteousness of one the free gift came upon all men unto justification of life. For as by one man's disobedience many were made sinners, so by the obedience of one shall many be made righteous.

Christ is that "one man." He is the firstborn. Christ Jesus fulfilled every prophecy, including each verse of Exodus 12 in which God gave the Passover instructions to the children of Israel.

6. One Passover lamb was offered for each house.

Exodus 12:3–4 points to an amazing principle foretold during the Passover, then fulfilled through the Lamb of God:

Speak ye unto all the congregation of Israel, saying, In the tenth day of this month they shall take to them every man a lamb, according to the house of their fathers, a lamb for an house: And if the household be too little for the lamb, let him and his neighbour next unto his house take it according to the number of the souls; every man according to his eating shall make your count for the lamb.

God's intention, from the first Passover, was a lamb sacrificed for each house. The shed blood was to cover every person in the household. It wasn't just the father, but fathers. It wasn't just the mother, but mothers. The protection included uncles, aunts, and cousins.

Certainly, every person in the household had the free choice of whether to stay in the house which was protected by the blood, just as each individual in a house has a free will to decide whether to accept

Jesus Christ as Savior. However, it is God's desire to protect the entire household. And this principle didn't start with the Passover. Even back in Genesis 7:1, the Bible declares, "*And the* LORD *said unto Noah, Come thou and all thy house into the ark; for thee have I seen righteous before me in this generation.*

In Joshua 24:15, we read:

> *And if it seem evil unto you to serve the* LORD, *choose you this day whom ye will serve; whether the gods which your fathers served that were on the other side of the flood, or the gods of the Amorites, in whose land ye dwell: but as for me and my house, we will serve the* LORD.

Acts 16:14–15 shares the story of Lydia, a new believer in Jesus:

> *And a certain woman named Lydia, a seller of purple, of the city of Thyatira, which worshiped God, heard us: whose heart the Lord opened, that she attended unto the things which were spoken of Paul. And when she was baptized, and her household, she besought us, saying, If ye have judged me to be faithful to the Lord, come into my house, and abide there. And she constrained us.*

Recorded later in that same chapter, the Philippian jailer, became not only a new believer, but also witnessed the miracle of household salvation:

> *Sirs, what must I do to be saved? And they said, Believe on the Lord Jesus Christ, and thou shalt be saved, and thy house. And they spake unto him the word of the Lord, and to all that were in his house. And he took them the same hour of the night, and washed their stripes; and was baptized, he and all his, straightway. And*

when he had brought them into his house, he set meat before them,
and rejoiced, believing in God with all his house. (Acts 16:30–34)

Acts 18:8 shares a similar account: *"And Crispus, the chief ruler of the synagogue, believed on the Lord with all his house; and many of the Corinthians hearing believed, and were baptized."*

Because of the principle of a lamb for a house, you have the legal right to claim every member of your family for Christ. The promise is yours. There is an umbrella of grace over you and your household.

When you become a believer, those closest to you cannot help but see the change that begins to happen supernaturally. They may run from the Lord. They may scoff at His Word. But they will be won to Christ Jesus because of the grace of God that rests on your household through the blood of the Lamb.

How do I know? I believe in this revelation with my whole heart because I have experienced it. After I accepted Jesus Christ in my life, God began moving in my family. First came my sister, then two brothers. Then my mom and dad were born again, and later the whole family. Hallelujah for this wonderful promise and provision that was revealed through the Passover and fulfilled on the cross!

7. Jesus, as the Passover lamb, was killed between two evenings.

The English translation of Exodus 12:6 is given this way: *"And ye shall keep it up until the fourteenth day of the same month: and the whole assembly of the congregation of Israel shall kill it in the evening."* The literal Hebrew translation for "evening" is "between two evenings."

Now, isn't it amazing, when you dig deeply into the treasures of the Bible, you find that the Lamb of God died between two evenings?

Look in Mark 15:33, which illuminates our understanding of what happened: *"And when the sixth hour was come, there was darkness over the whole land until the ninth hour."* He was nailed to Calvary's tree at nine in the morning. At twelve noon, which the Jews referred to as the sixth hour, something strange happened. Darkness came over the land and it lasted until three in the afternoon, or the ninth hour, the hour our Master died.

He literally fulfilled the prophecy in Exodus 12:5 and died between the first and second evening, or darkness, for after His death, the sun rose again, and then the sun set again at the regular hour.

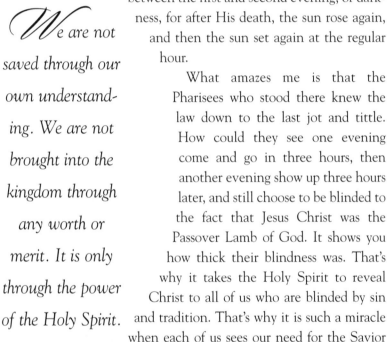

We are not saved through our own understanding. We are not brought into the kingdom through any worth or merit. It is only through the power of the Holy Spirit.

What amazes me is that the Pharisees who stood there knew the law down to the last jot and tittle. How could they see one evening come and go in three hours, then another evening show up three hours later, and still choose to be blinded to the fact that Jesus Christ was the Passover Lamb of God. It shows you how thick their blindness was. That's why it takes the Holy Spirit to reveal Christ to all of us who are blinded by sin and tradition. That's why it is such a miracle when each of us sees our need for the Savior and believes on Him.

We are not saved through our own understanding. We are not brought into the kingdom through any worth or merit. It is only through the power of the Holy Spirit: *"And you hath he quickened, who were dead in trespasses and sins"* (Ephesians 2:1).

It's so important to realize that your salvation is the greater miracle! It is greater than raising the dead, greater than making the sun stand still, and greater than the cleansing of lepers. Your salvation is life's greatest miracle, for it was given by God the Father in fulfillment of all the Scriptures, down to the smallest prophecy and promise.

Because of the miracle of salvation, you no longer have to live in spiritual darkness. You are no longer subject to Satan. Your name is listed no more among the damned but is written in the Lamb's Book of Life. When you were saved, with the swivel of His hand, God moved every demon away from you so you could see the light. In fact, your salvation was a greater miracle than the raising of Lazarus. It was a greater miracle than when Joshua asked God to make the sun stand still. Your salvation, just yours, is greater than all the miracles in the Bible. To Jesus be the glory and honor!

8. The whole assembly killed the Passover lamb.

We read it in Exodus 12:6: *"And ye shall keep it up until the fourteenth day of the same month: and the whole assembly of the congregation of Israel shall kill it in the evening."* When they gathered at Passover, the lamb was killed by every house in Israel. The children of Israel were told to memorialize that action in every Passover Feast to come.

Matthew 27:24–25 contains these startling words:

> *When Pilate saw that he could prevail nothing, but that rather a tumult was made, he took water, and washed his hands before the multitude, saying, I am innocent of the blood of this just person: see ye to it. Then answered all the people, and said, His blood be on us, and on our children.*

Those words were prophetic in two ways. First, for rejecting Christ, the nation of Israel has suffered unbearably during the past twenty centuries. Who can argue with that? However, another side of those prophetic words mean that His precious blood rests on them and their descendents. The blood of Jesus remains upon the Jewish people. One day soon, His blood shall save the whole house of Israel:

> *For this is the covenant that I will make with the house of Israel after those days, saith the Lord; I will put my laws into their mind, and write them in their hearts: and I will be to them a God, and they shall be to me a people: And they shall not teach every man his neighbour, and every man his brother, saying, Know the Lord: for all shall know me, from the least to the greatest. For I will be merciful to their unrighteousness, and their sins and their iniquities will I remember no more.* (Hebrews 8:10–12)

Oh, I cannot wait for the time when the great move of the Holy Spirit blows over the land of Israel. When it happens, can you imagine the celebration that will erupt in heaven? God loves His chosen people more than any of us will ever know this side of heaven. The day will come when the greatest move of God is going to take place in Israel. I believe we will be watching from heaven.

9. The blood was applied to the lintel and both door posts.

Exodus 12:7 describes in perfect detail what the children of Israel were to do with the shed blood: "*And they shall take of the blood, and strike it on the two side posts and on the upper door post of the houses.*"

Later in that same chapter, Moses gives even more detailed instructions:

> *And ye shall take a bunch of hyssop, and dip it in the blood that is in the bason, and strike the lintel and the two side posts with the blood that is in the bason; and none of you shall go out at the door of his house until the morning. For the LORD will pass through to*

smite the Egyptians; and when he seeth the blood upon the lintel, and on the two side posts, the LORD will pass over the door, and will not suffer the destroyer to come in unto your houses to smite you. (Exodus 12:22–23)

The door post and lintels are a perfect picture of the cross:

And they took Jesus, and led him away. And he bearing his cross went forth into a place called the place of a skull, which is called in the Hebrew Golgotha: where they crucified him. (John 19:16–18)

Add Hebrews 9:8–14 to those three passages of Scripture:

The Holy Ghost this signifying, that the way into the holiest of all was not yet made manifest, while as the first tabernacle was yet standing: Which was a figure for the time then present, in which were offered both gifts and sacrifices, that could not make him that did the service perfect, as pertaining to the conscience; which stood only in meats and drinks, and divers washings, and carnal ordinances, imposed on them until the time of reformation. But Christ being come an high priest of good things to come, by a greater and more perfect tabernacle, not made with hands, that is to say, not of this building; Neither by the blood of goats and calves, but by his own blood he entered in once into the holy place, having obtained eternal redemption for us. For if the blood of bulls and of goats, and the ashes of an heifer sprinkling the unclean, sanctifieth to the purifying of the flesh: How much more shall the blood of Christ, who through the eternal Spirit offered himself without spot to God, purge your conscience from dead works to serve the living God?

You see, communion is not a mere tradition that Christians tack on meaninglessly at the end of a service. It is important to know that we partake of the bread and cup to remember Him, all He has done, and all He desires to do through us.

The promises in Exodus belong to you, dear believer! The provisions of both the Old and New Covenants are yours. Jesus is the Lamb of God, yet He is also the blood-sprinkled door. The marks of the cross were still on Him when He rose from the grave and will remind us of what He did throughout all eternity:

> *And after eight days again his disciples were within, and Thomas with them: then came Jesus, the doors being shut, and stood in the midst, and said, Peace be unto you. Then saith he to Thomas, Reach hither thy finger, and behold my hands; and reach hither thy hand, and thrust it into my side: and be not faithless, but believing. And Thomas answered and said unto him, My Lord and my God.* (John 20:26–28)

Oh, that we would realize, alongside Thomas, that the hands, feet, and body of the crucified Christ were offered as a sacrifice that we might fall at His feet and say, "My Lord and my God."

The moment you apply the blood of Jesus to you and your family, the plagues cannot come. The destroyer cannot touch you. With the blood of Jesus comes protection and power. With the blood sprinkled freely comes hope, faith, love, and strength to serve Him daily. Only the blood of Jesus can save you, heal you, and keep you. What a revelation, for it spans the ages!

10. The Passover lamb was to be eaten in haste.

Exodus 12:8–11 states:

> *And they shall eat the flesh in that night, roast with fire, and unleavened bread; and with bitter herbs they shall eat it. Eat not of*

it raw, nor sodden at all with water, but roast with fire; his head with his legs, and with the purtenance thereof. And ye shall let nothing of it remain until the morning; and that which remaineth of it until the morning ye shall burn with fire. And thus shall ye eat it; with your loins girded, your shoes on your feet, and your staff in your hand; and ye shall eat it in haste: it is the LORD's passover.

When we understand this passage, we will understand communion (which is also called the Lord's Supper). Look at Matthew 26:26–28:

And as they were eating, Jesus took bread, and blessed it, and brake it, and gave it to the disciples, and said, Take, eat; this is my body. And he took the cup, and gave thanks, and gave it to them, saying, Drink ye all of it; for this is my blood of the new testament, which is shed for many for the remission of sins.

Let's look at two things included in these passages:

• **The meal was eaten in haste.** There was no need to stay in Egypt when they received deliverance. Egypt today is a wonderful country, of course, filled with many believers who are spreading the gospel throughout the nation. During the time of deliverance for the children of Israel, however, Egypt represented slavery and bondage, and it is still a spiritual symbol of the same. Egypt was filled then with gods that oppressed the people. Egypt's authority kept the children of Israel away from God's guidance. So when it was time to go, eating in haste meant the difference between death and life, staying versus leaving, bondage and freedom. We should learn this basic lesson instead of clinging to the life that kept us bound in sin. When it's time to go, go!

That is the reason why the Lord commanded us to be baptized, which is our public confession of death to this world, and to allow the Holy Spirit to raise us to a new life in Jesus Christ.

While I'm on the subject, let me mention why there are questions sometimes concerning the Feast of Passover and the Feast of Unleavened Bread and why they are often used interchangeably. For starters, they are in the same season of Passover. Even more, the Feast of Unleavened Bread mentioned in Exodus 12:11 was fulfilled when God commanded Israel to eat it and leave in haste. During the exodus from Egypt, the people ate the lamb, applied the blood, then left Egypt, fulfilling the Feast of Unleavened Bread as they left. Think about it: They applied the blood, the angel of death passed, they ate the lamb, and then before they could cook and eat the bread which had to be eaten at the same time, God said, "Go!" The children of Israel walked out of Egypt with the dough still fresh and uncooked. The reason today why so many believers are powerless and defeated is because they simply refuse to leave Egypt in haste.

It's time to realize that all the benefits of salvation can be ours if we stop lingering in Egypt. There is no time to stay in the world, no matter how attractive it is.

• **During the Passover Feast, three things were consumed.** The Israelites ate the body of the lamb which was roasted by fire, then the unleavened bread and the bitter herbs. In communion, we partake of the bread and the cup. In the study of the Feast of Unleavened Bread (chapter 3), I'll go deeper into this teaching and share how the bitter herbs, which represent the suffering of Christ, are a part of communion.

11. **As with Passover and the children of Israel, the Lamb of God allows us to pass from death to life.**

Let me invite you to read Exodus 12:11–13 with new eyes:

> And thus shall ye eat it; with your loins girded, your shoes on your feet, and your staff in your hand; and ye shall eat it in haste: it is

the LORD'S passover. For I will pass through the land of Egypt this night, and will smite all the firstborn in the land of Egypt, both man and beast; and against all the gods of Egypt I will execute judgment: I am the LORD. And the blood shall be to you for a token upon the houses where ye are: and when I see the blood, I will pass over you, and the plague shall not be upon you to destroy you, when I smite the land of Egypt.

Now look at Romans 3:24–25:

Being justified freely by his grace through the redemption that is in Christ Jesus: Whom God hath set forth to be a propitiation through faith in his blood, to declare his righteousness for the remission of sins that are past, through the forbearance of God.

Because of the blood of the lamb, the children of Israel passed from death to life, darkness to light. Because of the blood of the Lamb, believers today are also delivered from death to life. Judgment may be all around you, but the moment you experience salvation through the Cross, the blood of the Lamb covers your life. You are no longer under judgment. You are under grace because of the work of substitution in Christ Jesus. Because of the Cross, you no longer belong to Satan's domain.

Because of the blood of the lamb, the children of Israel passed from death to life, darkness to light.

There is an old chorus with these words:

This world is not my home; I'm just a-passing through.
My treasures are laid up somewhere beyond the blue.

The angels beckon me from heaven's open door,
And I can't feel at home in this world anymore.

Those words ring more true today than ever! Heaven has chosen you, so you cannot live as though you are still part of the world. As you follow Jesus, you will be surprised by what happens in the spirit. You begin to despise the things of the world and what they represent. The moment you experience the Savior in your heart, this world is no longer your home. You have passed from death to life. Your home is now heaven. And heaven will become sweeter and more inviting the longer you serve the Master.

12. The Passover, like communion, is a memorial.

Exodus 12:14 relates the meaning of the Passover: *"And this day shall be unto you for a memorial; and ye shall keep it a feast to the LORD throughout your generations; ye shall keep it a feast by an ordinance for ever."*
Matthew 26:26–28 shares an even more vital memorial:

> And as they were eating, Jesus took bread, and blessed it, and brake it, and gave it to the disciples, and said, Take, eat; this is my body. And he took the cup, and gave thanks, and gave it to them, saying, Drink ye all of it; For this is my blood of the new testament, which is shed for many for the remission of sins.

Likewise, the memorial is expressed in Luke 22:19–20:

> And he took bread, and gave thanks, and brake it, and gave unto them, saying, This is my body which is given for you: this do in remembrance of me. Likewise also the cup after supper, saying, This cup is the new testament in my blood, which is shed for you.

God told Moses the Passover observance would be a memorial. Communion, likewise, is a memorial to the work of the Cross. Even more importantly, we partake of the Lamb, Christ Jesus, and as we do, we receive health as we celebrate the communion. For the communion is not only the remembrance of the Cross, but it is the communion of Christ with His church. We experience union in the communion!

13. The Passover, like communion, is given for generations to come.

Also in Exodus 12:14, we are told that Passover should be observed throughout the generations. First Corinthians 11:26 illuminates the necessity to continue this observance until Jesus Christ returns for His church: *"For as often as ye eat this bread, and drink this cup, ye do shew the Lord's death till he come."*

14. Not a bone was broken.

According to Exodus 12:46, explicit directions were given concerning the care of the Passover lamb: *"In one house shall it be eaten; thou shalt not carry forth ought of the flesh abroad out of the house; neither shall ye break a bone thereof."*

Isn't it amazing how precise those directions were, especially in light of what happened to the Lamb of God on Calvary's cross?

David, with foresight and vision that could only have come from the inspiration of the Holy Spirit, wrote these words a thousand years before Christ came to earth: *"He keepeth all his bones: not one of them is broken"* (Psalm 34:20).

John 19:33 explains exactly what happened on the cross: *"But when they came to Jesus, and saw that he was dead already, they brake not his legs."*

The Lamb was to be offered without blemish and perfect, which certainly meant that no legs could be broken. The most amazing thing is that Christ died on the cross before the Roman soldiers had a chance to break His legs and cause almost instantaneous suffocation and death. Traditionally, that's what the soldiers did after a crucifixion.

Thank God for the Lamb of God who offered Himself—battered, bruised, bloody, but with no broken bones—as a perfect ransom for mankind's sins. What an amazing revelation!

15. There was safety only in the house under the protection of blood.

Exodus 12:22–24 points to the safety that only came through staying in the right place:

> And ye shall take a bunch of hyssop, and dip it in the blood that is in the bason [basin], and strike the lintel and the two side posts with the blood that is in the bason; and none of you shall go out at the door of his house until the morning. For the LORD will pass through to smite the Egyptians; and when he seeth the blood upon the lintel, and on the two side posts, the LORD will pass over the door, and will not suffer the destroyer to come in unto your houses to smite you. And ye shall observe this thing for an ordinance to thee and to thy sons for ever.

Hyssop is a plant that is still grown throughout the Middle East today and is symbolic of faith and purity in the Word of God. David prayed to God, "*Purge me with hyssop, and I shall be clean: wash me, and I shall be whiter than snow*" (Psalm 51:7). The children of Israel were commanded to take a branch of hyssop, and by faith, to apply the blood on the lintel and two side posts of their houses.

And so today our protection as believers is found only under the blood, through faith, for only under the precious blood of Christ Jesus are we free and safe from the Enemy. Hebrews 9:14–15 declares that because of the blood and the work of the Cross, we who are called will receive the promise of eternal inheritance which includes our protection.

16. During the Passover and because of the Cross, the enemy of God's children is spoiled.

Something remarkable happened in Egypt the night of the Passover. We read in Exodus 12:31–36:

> *And he called for Moses and Aaron by night, and said, Rise up, and get you forth from among my people, both ye and the children of Israel; and go, serve the LORD, as ye have said. Also take your flocks and your herds, as ye have said, and be gone; and bless me also. And the Egyptians were urgent upon the people, that they might send them out of the land in haste; for they said, We be all dead men. And the people took their dough before it was leavened, their kneadingtroughs being bound up in their clothes upon their shoulders. And the children of Israel did according to the word of Moses; and they borrowed of the Egyptians jewels of silver, and jewels of gold, and raiment: And the LORD gave the people favor in the sight of the Egyptians, so that they lent unto them such things as they required. And they spoiled the Egyptians.*

The Enemy was spoiled! So it is that Christ spoiled principalities and powers in His triumph on the cross. Look what the apostle Paul wrote in Colossians 2:10, 15: "*And ye are complete in him, which is the head of all principality and power.... And having spoiled principalities and powers, he made a shew of them openly, triumphing over them in it.*"

Because He spoiled the enemy of our soul, we partake in these spoils and His victory:

> *And I will restore to you the years that the locust hath eaten, the cankerworm, and the caterpiller, and the palmerworm.... And ye shall eat in plenty, and be satisfied, and praise the name of the LORD your God, that hath dealt wondrously with you: and my people shall never be ashamed.* (Joel 2:25–26)

17. Both the Passover and the work of the Cross provide a holy convocation, or a supernatural rest.

Exodus 12:16 proclaims: *"And in the first day there shall be an holy convocation, and in the seventh day there shall be an holy convocation to you; no manner of work shall be done in them, save that which every man must eat, that only may be done of you."*

Recorded later in that same chapter of Exodus are these words: *"And it shall come to pass, when ye be come to the land which the LORD will give you, according as he hath promised, that ye shall keep this service"* (12:25).

Observing the Passover season, the children of Israel were commanded to start and end the feast with rest, and to continue to observe that rest in the Promised Land.

A similar promise was given in Hebrews 4:1: *"Let us therefore fear, lest, a promise being left us of entering into his rest, any of you should seem to come short of it."* Rest was offered to believers, but a warning was also issued at the same time. We are commanded to seek supernatural rest in the Lamb of God, but only through faith and obedience can we receive it.

So Hebrews 4:1 declares that we are to experience God's rest because of the Cross. The work of Calvary brings us into our Sabbath. We cease from our work and rest in Him. Remember, on the cross Jesus our Redeemer said, *"It is finished"* (John 19:30).

The work of the Cross is finished, but faith in the work of the Lamb must always keep growing and building: *"There remaineth therefore a rest to the people of God"* (Hebrews 4:9).

18. The blood shall never lose its power.

As just mentioned in Exodus 12:25, God commanded Israel to keep the Passover continually and to apply the blood even after coming into the Promised Land. And so it is with us. The blood of Jesus must be applied continually on our lives. Our redemption is a daily dying to self and the world, as well as a daily cleansing in His precious blood: *"But if we walk in the light, as he is in the light, we have fellowship one with another, and the blood of Jesus Christ his Son, cleanseth us from all sin"* (1 John 1:7).

Zechariah 9:11 tells us: *"As for thee also, by the blood of thy covenant I have sent forth thy prisoners out of the pit wherein is no water."*

And only because of the blood are we free from the prison of sin and death. Hallelujah! The blood truly will never lose its power.

19. No outsider was allowed to celebrate the victories of deliverance, nor to partake of the Lamb.

Exodus 12:43 declares: *"And the LORD said unto Moses and Aaron, This is the ordinance of the passover: There shall no stranger eat thereof."*

First Corinthians 10:21 explains: *"Ye cannot drink the cup of the Lord, and the cup of devils: ye cannot be partakers of the Lord's table and of the table of devils."* This is why we are commanded to have no fellowship with unbelievers, but to *"come out from among them, and be ye separate, saith the Lord, and touch not the unclean thing; and I will receive you"* (2 Corinthians 6:17). The enemies of the gospel have no right to the Lord's Table. Only those redeemed and washed by His blood have that honor and privilege.

20. The Passover, as with the Cross, provided salvation and healing.

In Psalm 105:36–37, David recounts what happened because of the Passover: *"He smote also all the firstborn in their land, the chief of all their strength. He brought them forth also with silver and gold: and there was not one feeble person among their tribes."*

Now look in 2 Chronicles 30:

> *And there assembled at Jerusalem much people to keep the feast of unleavened bread in the second month, a very great congregation.… Then they killed the passover on the fourteenth day of the second month…the priests sprinkled the blood, which they received of the hand of the Levites.…But Hezekiah prayed for them, saying, The good LORD pardon every one That prepareth his heart to seek God, the LORD God of his fathers, though he be not cleansed according to the purification of the sanctuary. And the LORD hearkened to Hezekiah, and healed the people.* (verses 13, 15, 16, 18–20)

The Word of God teaches clearly that there is healing in the atonement, for every time we see the cross, we receive healing for our bodies. Isaiah 53:4–5 tells us:

> *Surely he hath borne our griefs, and carried our sorrows: yet we did esteem him stricken, smitten of God, and afflicted. But he was wounded for our transgressions, he was bruised for our iniquities: the chastisement of our peace was upon him; and with his stripes we are healed.*

First Peter 2:24 relates, *"Who his own self bare our sins in his own body on the tree, that we, being dead to sins, should live unto righteousness: by whose stripes ye were healed."*

So claim the benefits of the Cross today, for by His stripes we were healed. Healing is yours today!

21. The Passover brought praise.

The Word of God tells us in Exodus 15 that after Israel celebrated the Passover and crossed the Red Sea, they praised the Lord and sang:

> *I will sing unto the* LORD, *for he hath triumphed gloriously: the horse and his rider hath he thrown into the sea. The* LORD *is my strength and song, and he is become my salvation: he is my God, and I will prepare him an habitation; my father's God, and I will exalt him. The* LORD *is a man of war: the* LORD *is his name.* (Exodus 15:1–3)

Our salvation is the reason for our praise. The psalmist tells us:

> *And he brought forth his people with joy, and his chosen with gladness: And gave them the lands of the heathen: and they inherited the labour of the people: That they might observe his statutes, and keep his laws. Praise ye the* LORD." (Psalm 105:43–45)

A Final Note

The feasts in Israel were observed, in Christ fulfilled, and in each believer applied! We must apply them.

What a wonderful Savior we serve. He has revealed Himself to us from beginning to end. And each revelation from the Cross provides treasures untold. He knew each of us from the beginning of time, gave His life as a ransom for many, rose from the grave in victorious conquest, and now is preparing a glorious place in heaven for you and me.

3

THE LAMB OF GOD:
7 FEASTS OF ISRAEL

Repent ye therefore, and be converted, that your sins may be blotted out, when the times of refreshing shall come from the presence of the Lord; And he shall send Jesus Christ, which before was preached unto you: Whom the heaven must receive until the times of restitution of all things, which God hath spoken by the mouth of all his holy prophets since the world began.

—ACTS 3:19–21

As PART OF THE EXODUS FROM EGYPT, recorded in Exodus 12, God instituted seven feasts. In Leviticus 23, God additionally instructed the children of Israel to hold seven holy gatherings each year, celebrated during three feast seasons.

As we discussed previously, the feasts fall into three clusters. The first three feasts—Passover, Unleavened Bread, and Firstfruits—occur in rapid succession in the spring of the year over a period of eight days. Referred to collectively as "Passover," its purpose was to teach the children of Israel how to find and enter God's rest.

The fourth, Feast of Weeks, occurs fifty days later at the beginning of the summer. By New Testament times this feast had come to be known by its Greek name, Pentecost, a word meaning "fifty."

The last three gatherings, the Feast of Trumpets, Day of Atonement, and Feast of Tabernacles extend over a period of twenty-one days in the fall of the year. They are known collectively as "Tabernacles."

Each of these feasts was extremely significant for Israel, and they honored God for what He had done. Yet, it is important to remember that every feast points us to the Son of God.

The feasts in Israel were observed, in Christ fulfilled, and in each believer applied. Passover, Unleavened Bread, Firstfruits and Pentecost were fulfilled in Christ. Trumpets is about to be fulfilled in Christ at the Second Coming. Atonement will be fulfilled in Christ when all of Israel shall be saved. Tabernacles will be fulfilled in the thousand-year reign of Christ when He dwells among His people.

The feasts in Israel were observed, in Christ fulfilled, and in each believer applied.

As a believer, Passover is your salvation. Unleavened Bread is your deliverance from sin. Firstfruit is your new life in Christ. Pentecost is the fulfillment of the baptism of the Holy Spirit. We're all waiting for Trumpets when this corruption shall put on incorruption. Atonement is your sanctification and perfection. Tabernacles is where we will reign with Him for a thousand years on earth.

In chapter 2, we studied Passover in depth. This chapter will move quickly through each of the other six feasts, digging deeply into God's eternal treasures which are especially vital for believers today.

The Feast of Unleavened Bread

Let's continue studying the Passover season, focusing now on the second feast. In Exodus 12:15–17, God gave Moses specific instructions about this observance:

> *Seven days shall ye eat unleavened bread; even the first day ye shall put away leaven out of your houses: for whosoever eateth leavened bread from the first day until the seventh day, that soul shall be cut off from Israel. And in the first day there shall be an holy convocation, and in the seventh day there shall be an holy convocation to you; no manner of work shall be done in them, save that which every man must eat, that only may be done of you. And ye shall observe the feast of unleavened bread; for in this selfsame day have I brought your armies out of the land of Egypt: therefore shall ye observe this day in your generations by an ordinance for ever.*

On the night of Passover, the children of Israel were instructed to kill the lamb which had been chosen on the tenth day of the first month. That lamb was put aside for four days, then killed on the fourteenth day. The Israelites began eating unleavened bread as the blood was applied to the door frames.

For seven days, from the fourteenth to the twenty-first days, the Jewish people cleansed their homes of all leaven. This is extremely important, since leaven (also called yeast) is a symbol of sin. God commanded Israel to remove the leaven.

And so our Master Jesus, through His shed blood on Calvary, destroyed the power of sin. He died to remove the spiritual leaven. He destroyed sin the moment His blood was shed. He destroyed sin by the power of His blood. We as believers can experience a life with no leaven. Sin should not have power over you. We are free because the blood has been shed.

The moment you come to the Cross, you legally receive power over sin. Romans 6:10–13 bears this out:

> *For in that he died, he died unto sin once: but in that he liveth, he liveth unto God. Likewise reckon ye also yourselves to be dead indeed unto sin, but alive unto God through Jesus Christ our Lord.*

Let not sin therefore reign in your mortal body, that ye should obey it in the lusts thereof. Neither yield ye your members as instruments of unrighteousness unto sin: but yield yourselves unto God, as those that are alive from the dead, and your members as instruments of righteousness unto God.

Because we are free, we are commanded not to allow leaven into our lives. Paul the apostle tells us:

Know ye not that a little leaven leaveneth the whole lump? Purge out therefore the old leaven, that ye may be a new lump, as ye are unleavened. For even Christ our passover is sacrificed for us: Therefore let us keep the feast, not with old leaven, neither with the leaven of malice and wickedness; but with the unleavened bread of sincerity and truth. (1 Corinthians 5:6–8)

We have a choice whether to allow leaven in our lives or not. Sin has been destroyed, but we have the key. We need not allow sin to have dominion over our lives. And as we live this life of victory, we are reminded that when Israel partook of the Passover, they ate the lamb, shed and applied its blood, and ate the unleavened bread, then were healed. So it is with us. As we partake of Christ, we are cleansed by His blood and leave sin behind; we, too, are healed.

Do you know one of the reasons why many people are not healed? Look in Exodus 12:8 where we see these glorious instructions: *"And they shall eat the flesh in that night, roast with fire, and unleavened bread; and with bitter herbs they shall eat it."*

Healing took place when the children of Israel ate the lamb, after applying the blood, and then ate the unleavened bread with bitter herbs. The unleavened bread brought healing when eaten properly with the lamb and herbs. Too often, though, we want to experience salvation through the Lamb, but we don't want to die to sin, for dying to sin is the eating of unleavened bread with bitter herbs.

How can God heal us when we hang on to sin, avoiding the unleavened bread and bitter herbs? How can He touch our bodies and provide healing when we enjoy sin? We're mocking Him.

Unleavened bread is vital to the overall understanding of God's plan for His people. We must continue to partake as a memorial of all that Christ did for us on the cross: *"And this day shall be unto you for a memorial; and ye shall keep it a feast to the LORD throughout your generations; ye shall keep it a feast by an ordinance for ever"* (Exodus 12:14).

How can God heal us when we hang on to sin, avoiding the unleavened bread and bitter herbs?

I believe the day will come when all who partake of the Lamb of God, unleavened bread of righteousness, and bitter herbs of death to self will be healed. We will then experience the fullness of the Feast of Unleavened Bread and the season of Passover!

FEAST OF FIRSTFRUITS

In Leviticus 23:10–12, we read:

> *Speak unto the children of Israel, and say unto them, When ye be come into the land which I give unto you, and shall reap the harvest thereof, then ye shall bring a sheaf of the firstfruits of your harvest unto the priest: And he shall wave the sheaf before the LORD, to be accepted for you: on the morrow after the sabbath the priest shall wave it. And ye shall offer that day when ye wave the sheaf an he*

lamb without blemish of the first year for a burnt offering unto the
LORD.

It's important to know that a sheaf in the Scriptures is symbolic of a person. A good example is Joseph's dream:

And Joseph dreamed a dream, and he told it his brethren: and they hated him yet the more. And he said unto them, Hear, I pray you, this dream which I have dreamed: For, behold, we were binding sheaves in the field, and, lo, my sheaf arose, and also stood upright; and, behold, your sheaves stood round about, and made obeisance to my sheaf. And his brethren said to him, Shalt thou indeed reign over us? or shalt thou indeed have dominion over us? And they hated him yet the more for his dreams, and for his words. (Genesis 37:5–8)

This also helps us to understand Psalm 126:6 better: "*He that goeth forth and weepeth, bearing precious seed, shall doubtless come again with rejoicing, bringing his sheaves with him.*"

When the Lord came to earth the first time, He was called the Man of Sorrows. He came weeping and bearing precious seed, preaching the Word and carrying our sins and burdens on the cross. But on His second coming, He will come bringing His sheaves, His redeemed, with Him.

Remember how God told the children of Israel that when they came to the Promised Land and reaped their harvest, they should bring a sheaf of firstfruits? Then they were to give it to the priest, and on the day after the Sabbath the priest would wave that sheaf before the Lord.

What is the Feast of Firstfruits? It is the resurrection of Christ Jesus. We know this because in 1 Corinthians 15:20, Paul tells us:

But now is Christ risen from the dead, and become the first fruits of them that slept. For since by man came death, by man came also

the resurrection of the dead. For as in Adam all die, even so in
Christ shall all be made alive. But every man in his own order:
Christ the firstfruits; afterward they that are Christ's at his coming.

Also, Exodus 23:19 points out an amazing truth concering what happened after the Word declares that the firstfruits were to be taken to the house of the Lord: *"The first of the firstfruits of thy land thou shalt bring into the house of the LORD thy God."* This revealed prophetically that Christ will ascend to heaven after His resurrection, and will then enter into the house of the Lord. This is why the book of Hebrews declares:

Now when these things were thus ordained, the priests went always
into the first tabernacle, accomplishing the service of God. But into the
second went the high priest alone once every year, not without blood,
which he offered for himself, and for the errors of the people: The Holy
Ghost this signifying, that the way into the holiest of all was not yet
made manifest, while as the first tabernacle was yet standing. (9:6–8)

The Feast of Pentecost

As you recall, the three Feasts of Passover, Unleavened Bread, and Firstfruits were all celebrated during the same season during the first month of the Jewish calendar. Remember, the first Passover season of feasts began during the Exodus and continued until the children of Israel reached the Red Sea. After passing miraculously through the waters and being led by a pillar of fire by night and a cloud by day, the children of Israel were brought to the foot of Mount Sinai. Here at Sinai, they experienced the Feast of Weeks, or Harvest, also called Pentecost, in the third month.

At Sinai, the Ten Commandments and law were given by God to Moses and the nation of Israel. Here the Lord gave instructions concerning the building of the tabernacle. Here the Aaronic priesthood was established. Here the sacrificial system was given. Here the nation of Israel was established in the wilderness as a forerunner of the church:

> He brought them out, after that he had shewed wonders and signs in the land of Egypt, and in the Red sea, and in the wilderness forty years. This is that Moses, which said unto the children of Israel, A prophet shall the Lord your God raise up unto you of your brethren, like unto me; him shall ye hear. This is he, that was in **the church in the wilderness** with the angel which spake to him in the mount Sina [Sinai], and with our fathers: who received the lively oracles to give unto us. (Acts 7:36–38, emphasis added)

The Greek name for this feast, as found in Leviticus 23:15–16, is Pentecost, meaning "fiftieth." That passage declares:

> And ye shall count unto you from the morrow after the sabbath, from the day that ye brought the sheaf of the wave offering; seven sabbaths shall be complete: Even unto the morrow after the seventh sabbath shall ye number fifty days; and ye shall offer a new meat offering unto the LORD.

The fifty days is very important. Remember, the Jewish calendar is based on the lunar cycle, so it is different from our Gregorian or Julian calendar, both based on the solar cycles. The Jewish calendar is eleven days shorter than a solar-based calendar.

Passover took place on the fourteenth day of the first month. Israel left on the fifteenth day at midnight. After fifteen days walking in the wilderness, then continuing through the desert during the second month, they continued four more days through the third month before coming to Mount Sinai:

- The first month, Abib, had fifteen days remaining after the Passover.

- The second month, Zif, had thirty days.

- The third month, Sivan, had four days before Pentecost.

- This equals forty-nine days, or seven weeks times seven days each.

The number fifty represents liberty, freedom, and deliverance. In fact, every fiftieth year in Israel is a year of Jubilee. It was established by God as a time of release and freedom. Slaves were set free. Debts were cancelled. Families were reunited (Leviticus 25:10–13, 18–19).

After crossing the Red Sea, the children of Israel came to Mount Sinai the first day of the third month. Moses was told to prepare the people, so he sanctified the people. Then the next day, fifty days after celebrating Passover and leaving Egypt, Moses went up the mountain. What happened next changed the nation of Israel forever:

> And it came to pass…there were thunders and lightnings, and a thick cloud upon the mount, and the voice of the trumpet exceeding loud; so that all the people that was in the camp trembled. And Moses brought forth the people out of the camp to meet with God; and they stood at the nether part of the mount. And mount Sinai was altogether on a smoke, because the LORD descended upon it in fire: and the smoke thereof ascended as the smoke of a furnace, and the whole mount quaked greatly. And when the voice of the trumpet sounded long, and waxed louder and louder, Moses spake, and God answered him by a voice. And the LORD came down upon mount Sinai, on the top of the mount: and the LORD called Moses up to the top of the mount; and Moses went up. (Exodus 19:16–20)

Then the Lord wrote the law with His finger and gave it to Moses to proclaim to the children of Israel. To this day, Israel celebrates the Feast of Pentecost, also called Weeks or Harvest, to commemorate the giving of the law.

The message is very clear. Christ Jesus, the resurrected Lamb of God, is the blood-sprinkled Door of salvation. You cannot enter into fellowship except through Him. Just as the Israelites walked through the Red Sea, believers today go through baptism. And what awaits us after baptism? Pentecost!

Just as Jesus was baptized and came out of the water, the Holy Ghost, in the form of a dove, rested on Christ Jesus. After the death and resurrection of the Savior, the apostles and believers in the book of Acts prepared themselves during the time of the Feast of Pentecost. What happened next changed the church of Jesus Christ forever:

> And when the day of Pentecost was fully come, they were all with one accord in one place. And suddenly there came a sound from heaven as of a rushing mighty wind, and it filled all the house where they were sitting. And there appeared unto them cloven tongues like as of fire, and it sat upon each of them. And they were all filled with the Holy Ghost, and began to speak with other tongues, as the Spirit gave them utterance. (Acts 2:1–4)

On the fiftieth day after the Lord and His disciples celebrated Passover, the apostles celebrated Pentecost in the Upper Room, and supernatural signs were again seen as in the first Pentecost when Moses received the Law. Fire descended, as in Exodus. And this time the law of God was written on the hearts of those present, rather than on tablets of stone. And after Peter preached the gospel on that glorious day, rather than 3,000 people being slain, as was the case on the first Pentecost (Exodus 32:28), 3,000 were wonderfully born again:

Then Peter said unto them, Repent, and be baptized every one of you in the name of Jesus Christ for the remission of sins, and ye shall receive the gift of the Holy Ghost…. Then they that gladly received his word were baptized: and the same day there were added unto them about three thousand souls. (Acts 2:38, 41)

And during the Feast of Weeks in the Old Covenant, God told the priest that they were to take two loaves of bread and put leaven in them. This is quite remarkable. He had forbidden Israel to eat leavened bread during the Passover season. But during the feast that we now call Pentecost, He told the priest to have two loaves full of leaven:

And ye shall count unto you from the morrow after the sabbath, from the day that ye brought the sheaf of the wave offering; seven sabbaths shall be complete: Even unto the morrow after the seventh sabbath shall ye number fifty days; and ye shall offer a new meat offering unto the LORD. *Ye shall bring out of your habitations two wave loaves of two tenth deals: they shall be of fine flour; they shall be baken with leaven; they are the firstfruits unto the* LORD. (Leviticus 23:15–17)

Since leaven represents sin, why would God require leaven or something representing sin in those loaves being waved before Him during this feast?

The Passover pointed to Christ Jesus and His sinless life, so leaven was not allowed during this season, from the very first time it was celebrated. But the Feast of Weeks pointed toward Pentecost, which focuses on the people of God, the church, which has not yet attained sinlessness or perfection. Leaven in the two waved loaves of the Feast of Pentecost shows God's recognition that the root of sin has not yet been removed, even though the believer is indwelt by the Holy Spirit. The two loaves were prophetic, yet Israel could not see it.

Of what do the two loaves speak? What happened at Pentecost? Jews and Gentiles alike were permitted to receive the Holy Spirit, even though both were still in a natural state of sin and imperfection. God was willing to pour the Holy Spirit into earthen vessels.

Do you want to know something also very exciting concerning Pentecost? Look in Leviticus 23:17: *"Ye shall bring out of your habitations two wave loaves of two tenth deals: they shall be of fine flour; they shall be baken with leaven; they are the first fruits unto the LORD."*

Notice the two-tenths of fine flour. According to calculations by some Bible scholars, the manna which fell from heaven had two-tenth deals of flour in it. (According to Exodus 16:36, each omer had a tenth part of flour, and on the Sabbath they were instructed to gather two omers, consisting of two-tenths of flour, which points to the double-portion anointing!) The meal offering presented on the feast day of Firstfruits (which pointed to the resurrection of Jesus Christ) was also made with a two-tenth deal of fine flour: *"And the meat offering thereof shall be two tenth deals of fine flour mingled with oil, an offering made by fire unto the LORD for a sweet savour: and the drink offering thereof shall be of wine, the fourth part of an hin"* (Leviticus 23:13). Likewise, the twelve loaves of shewbread in the Holy Place of the tabernacle also were made with two-tenths of fine flour: *"And thou shalt take fine flour, and bake twelve cakes thereof: two tenth deals shall be in one cake"* (Leviticus 24:5–7).

These consistencies throughout the Bible must point to something very special, but what? As with manna gathered for the Sabbath, the double portion is always connected to the two-tenth deal of fine flour. God told Moses to use these loaves during the Feast of Pentecost, and the loaves represented Jews and Gentiles. The unleavened bread pointed to imperfect people who would receive the Holy Spirit during Pentecost after the resurrection. And the two-tenth deals of fine flour in these loaves should tell believers throughout the ages that God legally permitted a double portion. God not only sent the Holy Spirit that day, but He promised and gave a double portion of the Holy Spirit.

These loaves weren't small. According to Mishna, the writings of the oral law that have been handed down in Jewish culture through the centuries, each loaf would have been twenty-eight inches long, sixteen inches wide, and seven inches tall. A double portion of these would have been quite a heavy offering.

With that in mind, look in verse 20 of Leviticus 23 at something else that should give you even more reason to rejoice: *"And the priest shall wave them with the bread of the first fruits for a wave offering before the* Lord." The word "wave" in Hebrew is *tunufa*. It means "to vibrate." It literally means "to sway in vibration," "to quiver," "to rock to and fro." In other words, the priest was to vibrate, to sway, and to quiver the two loaves before the Lord during the feast. As mentioned, these were heavy loaves. Vibrating them would have been very demonstrative, certainly quite apparent. And that's exactly what happened in the Upper Room during the Day of Pentecost when the Holy Spirit *"filled all the house"* (Acts 2:2), so much so that some observers mocked, saying, *"These men are full of new wine"* (Acts 2:13).

I have news for you. If you see people shaking under the anointing of the Holy Spirit, they're doing nothing different than the priests did in *tunufa* before the Lord. The Holy Spirit is not given without action, without a manifestation. The most quiet, conservative Christians, when they truly receive the Holy Spirit, will often experience a glorious manifestation. And when the Holy Spirit is moving upon a life, there is always beauty and perfection. The baptism in the Holy Spirit is life-changing and powerful beyond description. It must be experienced to be understood. Mere words fall far short.

But, my brother and sister, let me emphasize that no one can receive this glorious experience until first coming to the Cross and being washed in the blood of the Lamb (Passover), forsaking sin and the world (Unleavened Bread), and being risen to newness of life (Firstfruits).

THE COMING SEASON OF TABERNACLES

The first season of feasts was called Passover. The second season, a single feast called Pentecost, or Weeks, came next. The third and final feast season, Tabernacles, has always been the most glorious season of all. It was the feast of all feasts to the children of Israel. This season has also been called the Feast of Prophecy, for the three parts of this season point specifically to coming events in this manner:

THE FEAST OF TRUMPETS

The season of tabernacles was introduced on the first day of the seventh month by the blowing of trumpets. It was a festival of trumpets, sounding throughout the land, and calling the nation to prepare for the coming day of national cleansing.

Psalm 89:15 declares, *"Blessed is the people that know the joyful sound: they shall walk, O Lord, in the light of thy countenance."* The first part of that verse can also be translated as "they that know the blast of the trumpet." This feast day is called the Day of Blowing of Trumpets, and the significance of trumpets in Israel should be understood.

First, there were two kinds of trumpets in Israel—trumpets made of rams' horns and trumpets made of silver. The rams' horns were used especially to blast out the note of shouting in the fall of the walls of Jericho (Joshua 6:5), and it was also the trumpet of the jubilee spoken of in Leviticus 25: *"Then shalt thou cause the trumpet of the jubile [jubilee] to sound on the tenth day of the seventh month, in the day of atonement shall ye make the trumpet sound throughout all your land"* (verse 9).

And the two silver trumpets were made for the various callings of Israel. Silver in the Scripture speaks of redemption (Exodus 30:11–16; Numbers 3:40–50; 10:2–3), for it was used as ransom for the atonement:

> When thou takest the sum of the children of Israel after their number, then shall they give every man a ransom for his soul unto the LORD, when thou numberest them; that there be no plague among them, when thou numberest them. This they shall give, every one that passeth among them that are numbered, half a shekel after the shekel of the sanctuary. (Exodus 30:12–13)

The trumpet, in Scripture, is also used to symbolize the prophetic voice. The prophets, for example, were told to lift up their voices like a trumpet: *"Cry aloud, spare not, lift up thy voice like a trumpet, and shew my people their transgression, and the house of Jacob their sins"* (Isaiah 58:1). Hosea 8:1 also instructs: *"Set the trumpet to thy mouth. He shall come as an eagle against the house of the LORD, because they have transgressed my covenant, and trespassed against my law."*

The trumpets in Israel were used for these primary reasons:

- **The calling of the assemblies:** *"And the Lord spake unto Moses, saying, Make thee two trumpets of silver; of a whole piece shalt thou make them: that thou mayest use them for the calling of the assembly, and for the journeying of the camps"* (Numbers 10:1–2).

- **The journeyings of the camp:** Also referenced in Numbers 10:2.

- **The blowing of alarms:** *"When ye blow an alarm, then the camps that lie on the east parts shall go forward. When ye blow an alarm the second time, then the camps that lie on the south side shall take their journey: they shall blow an alarm for their journeys. But when* *the congregation is to be gathered together, ye shall blow, but ye shall not sound an alarm"* (Numbers 10:5–7).

- **Wars:** *"I cannot hold my peace, because thou has heard, O my soul, the sound of the trumpet, the alarm of war"* (Jeremiah 4:19).

- **Offerings and sacrifices:** *"Also in the day of your gladness, and in your solemn days, and in the beginnings of your months, ye shall blow with the trumpets over your burnt offerings, and over the sacrifices of your peace offerings; that they may be to you for a memorial before your God: I am the LORD your God"* (Numbers 10:10).

- **The anointing of kings:** *"Then they hasted, and took every man his garment, and put it under him on the top of the stairs, and blew with trumpets, saying, Jehu is king"* (2 Kings 9:13).

- **Dedication of the temple of Solomon:** *"It came even to pass, as the trumpeters and singers were as one, to make one sound to be heard in praising and thanking the Lord; and when they lifted up their voice with the trumpets and cymbals and instruments of musick, and praised the Lord, saying, For he is good; for his mercy endureth for ever; that then the house was filled with a cloud, even the house of the Lord; So that the priests could not stand to minister by reason of the cloud: for the glory of the Lord had filled the house of God"* (2 Chronicles 5:13–14).

The trumpets will also be used in final judgments of God: *"And when he had opened the seventh seal, there was silence in heaven about the space of half an hour. And I saw the seven angels which stood before God; and to them were given seven trumpets"* (Revelation 8:1–2); and at the Second Coming of Jesus Christ: *"For the Lord himself shall descend from heaven with a shout, with the voice of the archangel, and with the trump of God: and the dead in Christ shall rise first"* (1 Thessalonians 4:16).

The Feast of Trumpets was ushered in by the blast of horns. That is why it was called the Day of the Blowing of Trumpets. And I believe that the Day of the Blowing of Trumpets will be fulfilled in the rapture of the church. First Corinthians 15:52 points to the great moment when the trumpet shall sound: *"In a moment, in the twinkling of an eye, at the last trump; for the trumpet shall sound, and the dead shall be raised incorruptible, and we shall be changed."*

The word *rapture* is a word we use for the phrase "caught up," which is found in 1 Thessalonians 4:17: *"Then we which are alive and remain shall be caught up together with them in the clouds, to meet the Lord in the air: and so shall we ever be with the Lord."*

And the Scripture tells us that when the Lord returns, He will come as a thief in the night: *"For yourselves know perfectly that the day of the Lord so cometh as a thief in the night"* (1 Thessalonians 5:2). I believe this glorious event is almost upon us, and it will happen in the twinkling of an eye. I've been told that the twinkling of an eye is eleven one-hundredths of a second. With blinding speed, we will be changed! Things are going to happen swiftly at the sound of the trumpet.

Paul tells us of that day. In 1 Corinthians 15:50–51, he states, *"Now this I say, brethren, that flesh and blood cannot inherit the kingdom of God; neither doth corruption inherit incorruption. Behold, I show you a mystery."*

The apostle is speaking of a hidden revelation. It is a truth that we need to understand. Paul continues, *"We shall not all sleep; but we shall all be changed, in a moment, in the twinkling of an eye, at the last trump"* (verses 51–52).

Jesus is coming back, and the Bible states that He will come for those who look for Him: *"So Christ was once offered to bear the sins of many; and unto them that look for him shall he appear the second time without sin unto salvation"* (Hebrews 9:28).

Now there is something that I want to help you understand. The Scriptures tell us that this glorious day will not come until there is a falling away first and the man of sin is revealed:

Now we beseech you, brethren, by the coming of our Lord Jesus Christ, and by our gathering together unto him, that ye be not soon shaken in mind, or be troubled, neither by spirit, nor by word, nor by letter as from us, as that the day of Christ is at hand. Let no man deceive you by any means: for that day shall not come, except there come a falling away first, and that man of sin be revealed, the son of perdition. (2 Thessalonians 2:1–3)

Later on in the same chapter, Paul tells us that the Holy Spirit, the Power keeping the antichrist from appearing, will be taken out of the way: *"For the mystery of iniquity doth already work: only he who now letteth will let, until he be taken out of the way. And then shall that Wicked be revealed, whom the Lord shall consume with the spirit of his mouth, and shall destroy with the brightness of his coming"* (verses 7–8).

Oh, beloved of God, when that happens, you and I are going to experience the greatest moment since our salvation! When the Holy Spirit leaves this world, you and I are going with Him. That is when the Rapture of 1 Corinthians 15:51–52 and 1 Thessalonians 4:17 will take place!

Also, it is important to know that you and I, as believers, will not go through the period the Bible calls the Great Tribulation or the time of wrath, for the Scripture declares: *"For God hath not appointed us to wrath, but to obtain salvation by our Lord Jesus Christ"* (1 Thessalonians 5:9).

Now remember, when God was about to destroy Sodom and Gomorrah, He first sent His angels to bring Lot out. In Genesis 19:22, the angel told Lot, *"Haste thee, escape thither; for I cannot do any thing till thou be come thither."* So it is clear from Scripture that God took the righteous out of the way before destruction came.

Also, in Isaiah 26:19, we read: *"Thy dead men shall live, together with my dead body shall they arise. Awake and sing, ye that dwell in dust: for thy dew is as the dew of herbs, and the earth shall cast out the dead."*

This was fulfilled when Christ Jesus rose from the dead, spoken of in Matthew 27:50–53:

Jesus, when he had cried again with a loud voice, yielded up the ghost. And, behold, the veil of the temple was rent in twain from the top to the bottom; and the earth did quake, and the rocks rent; And the graves were opened; and many bodies of the saints which slept arose, And came out of the graves after his resurrection, and went into the holy city, and appeared unto many.

Verse 20 of Isaiah 26 goes on to tell us: "*Come, my people, enter thou into thy chambers, and shut thy doors about thee: hide thyself as it were for a little moment, until the indignation be overpast.*"

This is the rapture of the church, for God will take His people to protect them from the destruction that will descend soon on planet Earth, as revealed in verse 21 of Isaiah 26: "*For, behold, the LORD cometh out of his place to punish the inhabitants of the earth for their iniquity: the earth also shall disclose her blood, and shall no more cover her slain.*" Think about it—there will be destruction so great there will not be enough graves to bury the dead.

Remember, the Scripture says God cannot judge the righteous with the wicked, for when Abraham was interceding for Sodom and Gomorrah, he prayed, "*That be far from thee to do after this manner, to slay the righteous with the wicked: and that the righteous should be as the wicked, that be far from thee: Shall not the Judge of all the earth do right?*" (Genesis 18:25).

That is why after Paul the apostle told the church in Thessalonica of that glorious day (1 Thessalonians 4:13–17), he concluded by telling them to comfort one another, for the rapture of the church is a message of hope and comfort, not fear and confusion. And the Lord Jesus told us to be ready for that day, for in Matthew 24:44, we read: "*Therefore be ye also ready: for in such an hour as ye think not the Son of man cometh.*"

So, beloved of God, "*look up, and lift up your heads; for your redemption draweth nigh*" (Luke 21:28).

DAY OF ATONEMENT

Now we come to the most solemn of all feasts. The Day of Atonement was the time for national and sanctuary cleansing. On this day sacrifices were offered for atonement or reconciliation. The special and peculiar offerings were those of the two goats:

> *And he shall take of the congregation of the children of Israel two kids of the goats for a sin offering, and one ram for a burnt offering. And Aaron shall offer his bullock of the sin offering, which is for himself, and make an atonement for himself, and for his house. And he shall take the two goats, and present them before the* LORD *at the door of the tabernacle of the congregation. And Aaron shall cast lots upon the two goats; one lot for the* LORD*, and the other lot for the scapegoat. And Aaron shall bring the goat upon which the* LORD*'s lot fell, and offer him for a sin offering.* (Leviticus 16:5–9)

One goat was slain, and the other was taken to the wilderness at the hand of a man, bearing away the sins of the people. It was on this day, which took place but once a year, the high priest entered into the holiest of all, within the veil, with the blood of the sin offering. Here he sprinkled the blood on the mercy seat. The blood of the sin offering on the great Day of Atonement brought about the cleansing of all sins, all iniquities, and all transgressions. The priesthood, the sanctuary, and Israel as a nation, experienced the atonement of the blood. That day, they were reconciled to God.

Leviticus 23:26–28 explains:

> *And the Lord spake unto Moses, saying, Also on the tenth day of this seventh month there shall be a day of atonement: it shall be an holy convocation unto you; and ye shall afflict your souls, and offer an offering made by fire unto the Lord. And ye shall do no work in*

that same day: for it is a day of atonement, to make an atonement for you before the Lord your God.

Numbers 29:7–11 also points to this solemn day:

And ye shall have on the tenth day of this seventh month an holy convocation; and ye shall afflict your souls: ye shall not do any work therein: But ye shall offer a burnt offering unto the LORD for a sweet savour; one young bullock, one ram, and seven lambs of the first year; they shall be unto you without blemish: And their meat offering shall be of flour mingled with oil, three tenth deals to a bullock, and two tenth deals to one ram, A several tenth deal for one lamb, throughout the seven lambs: One kid of the goats for a sin offering; beside the sin offering of atonement, and the continual burnt offering, and the meat offering of it, and their drink offerings.

It is important that we understand that the Day of Atonement has a threefold fulfillment:

1. **In Israel.** The Day of Atonement was the most solemn of all days throughout the land. God Almighty declares this through the prophet Zechariah, as written in chapter 3, verse 9: *"I will remove the iniquity of that land in one day."* The nation of Israel yearly observed the Day of Atonement, yet one of these days God will fulfill the promise of Zechariah when Israel will be saved.

2. **In Christ Jesus.** We must also clearly understand that this feast was fulfilled completely in the Person and ministry of our wonderful Lord Jesus when He was crucified on Calvary's cross and said, *"It is finished"* (John 19:30).

3. **In the believers, when we stand on that day clean and perfect.** Someday soon the feast will be fulfilled in us, the church. When we stand before Him and know the fullness of the manifestation of the power of His blood, which will destroy the power of sin forever, we will stand perfect before His throne, free at last from all iniquity, transgressions, and death.

Now, the Lord had commanded Aaron not to come into the Holiest of Holies at all times, but only on this one day of the year. Even then he was only to enter with the blood of the sacrifice, the golden censor, and his hands full of sweet incense. Only then could he bring the offering within the veil:

> And the LORD spake unto Moses after the death of the two sons of Aaron, when they offered before the LORD, and died; And the LORD said unto Moses, Speak unto Aaron thy brother, that he come not at all times into the holy place within the vail [veil] before the mercy seat, which is upon the ark; that he die not: for I will appear in the cloud upon the mercy seat…. And he shall take a censer full of burning coals of fire from off the altar before the LORD, and his hands full of sweet incense beaten small, and bring it within the vail: And he shall put the incense upon the fire before the LORD, that the cloud of the incense may cover the mercy seat that is upon the testimony, that he die not: And he shall take of the blood of the bullock, and sprinkle it with his finger upon the mercy seat eastward; and before the mercy seat shall he sprinkle of the blood with his finger seven times. Then shall he kill the goat of the sin offering, that is for the people, and bring his blood within the vail, and do with that blood as he did with the blood of the bullock, and sprinkle it upon the mercy seat, and before the mercy seat: And he shall make an

atonement for the holy place, because of the uncleanness of the chil-
dren of Israel, and because of their transgressions in all their sins:
and so shall he do for the tabernacle of the congregation, that remaineth
among them in the midst of their uncleanness. (Leviticus 16:1–2,
12–16)

Notice four wonderful parallels in the threefold fulfillment—Israel,
Christ Jesus, and the church—concerning the Day of Atonement:

The precious blood. First, Aaron came in with the blood of the
bullock, which he sprinkled seven times on the mercy seat. This was
fulfilled in the perfect work of the Cross when the blood of Jesus was
shed seven times for you and me:

1. The blood was first shed in Gethsemane from His lovely fore-
   head (Luke 22:44).
2. Then the blood was shed as they placed the crown of thorns
   upon his head (John 19:2).
3. The blood was shed as the soldiers smote His precious face
   (Matthew 26:67) and plucked off the hair of His beard (Isaiah
   50:6).
4. The Savior's blood was shed for the fourth time as His back
   was scourged (Matthew 27:26).
5. The next time came as the soldiers crucified Him, nailing His
   hands to the cross (Matthew 27:35; John 20:27).
6. His blood was shed as they nailed His feet to the cross (Luke
   24:39–40).
7. The final time came as His side was pierced (John 19:34).

Incense. As Aaron entered within the veil, placing the incense on
the fiery coals of the censor, a cloud of incense ascended, covering the

ark of glory. Incense always speaks of prayer and worship. David wrote in Psalm 141:2, *"Let my prayer be set forth before thee as incense; and the lifting up of my hands as the evening sacrifice."* This finds its fulfillment in Christ Jesus and the church, for He is the Mediator and Intercessor. Hebrews 7:25 states, *"Wherefore he is able also to save them to the uttermost that come unto God by him, seeing he ever liveth to make intercession for them."*

The incense also speaks of worship, for the Scripture says in Psalm 29:2, *"Give unto the Lord the glory due unto his name; worship the Lord in the beauty of holiness."* That will find its fulfillment when we stand before Him, holy, praising Him for all He has done.

Washing of water. On the Day of Atonement, also, there was the special washing of water in preparation for the sacrificial offering. Aaron washed before he entered the sanctuary, then washed again in the holy place after the sanctuary had been cleansed. Notice Leviticus 16:4 and 24:

> He shall put on the holy linen coat, and he shall have the linen
> breeches upon his flesh, and shall be girded with a linen girdle, and
> with the linen mitre shall he be attired: these are the holy garments;
> therefore shall he wash his flesh in water, and so put them on....
> And he shall wash his flesh with water in the holy place, and put on
> his garments, and come forth, and offer his burnt offering, and the
> burnt offering of the people, and make an atonement for himself,
> and for the people.

This will be fulfilled in the church on that glorious day, for Ephesians 5:26–27 declares: *"That he might sanctify and cleanse it with the washing of water by the word, That he might present it to himself a glorious church, not having spot, or wrinkle, or any such thing; but that it should be holy and without blemish."* On that day He will cleanse us with the water of the Word in order that He might present us to Himself!

Changing of the garments. On this day also, Aaron laid aside his garments of glory and beauty. Exodus 28 describes the beautiful clothing: *"And thou shalt make holy garments for Aaron thy brother for glory and for beauty"* (verse 2). Aaron laid aside those garments of glory and beauty, then put on linen garments: *"He shall put on the holy linen coat, and he shall have the linen breeches upon his flesh, and shall be girded with a linen girdle, and with the linen mitre shall he be attired: these are holy garments"* (Leviticus 16:4). After making the atonement in the sanctuary and washing the holy place, he took off the holy garments of linen and changed back into the garments of glory and beauty.

How wonderfully the Lord Jesus fulfilled this type in Himself, for He laid aside His reputation, emptying Himself of His glory, and took on the likeness of men:

> *Who, being in the form of God, thought it not robbery to be equal with God: But made himself of no reputation, and took upon him the form of a servant, and was made in the likeness of men: And being found in fashion as a man, he humbled himself, and became obedient unto death, even the death of the cross. Wherefore God also hath highly exalted him, and given him a name which is above every name.* (Philippians 2:6–9)

Later on, God highly exalted Him, clothed Him with glory and honor, and gave Him a name above all names! Likewise, on that soon-coming, glorious day, believers will also experience a change of garments when we put off this corruption and put on incorruption.

The word *atonement* means "reconciliation," and that day will bring full reconciliation between God and His people. The Day of Atonement, established as the most solemn of all feasts, was fulfilled in Christ Jesus when He died on Calvary's cross. That solemnity will be turned into celebration as we see the full manifestation of this feast!

What a day that will be when the power of the blood of Jesus Christ will bring us, the church, to perfection—making an end of all sin, all iniquity, all transgression-as we stand perfect in His glorious presence!

FEAST OF TABERNACLES

The final part of the Tabernacle season during the Jewish seventh month is the Feast of Tabernacles. Dating back to the time of Moses and the giving of the law, this feast was the most celebrated, for it signaled the end of the final harvest of the year and meant that the fruit harvest was all gathered. At this time, the children of Israel were to set aside seven days to the Lord. They were to leave their homes and dwell in booths made from tree leaves, rejoicing before God.

Oh, beloved, I pray that as you read the next few pages, the Holy Spirit will show you something glorious.

Look in Leviticus 23:33–36:

> And the LORD spake unto Moses, saying, Speak unto the children of Israel, saying, The fifteenth day of this seventh month shall be the feast of tabernacles for seven days unto the LORD. On the first day shall be an holy convocation: ye shall do no servile work therein. Seven days ye shall offer an offering made by fire unto the LORD: on the eighth day shall be an holy convocation unto you; and ye shall offer an offering made by fire unto the LORD: it is a solemn assembly; and ye shall do no servile work therein.

This feast, known as *Succoth* in Hebrew, was the Feast of Ingathering, referred to in Exodus 23:16, *"The feast of ingathering, which is in the end of the year, when thou hast gathered in thy labours out of the field."* It is also the solemn feast mentioned in Deuteronomy 16:15:

> *Seven days shalt thou keep a solemn feast unto the* LORD *thy God in the place which the* LORD *shall choose: because the* LORD *thy God shall bless thee in all thine increase, and in all the works of thine hands, therefore thou shalt surely rejoice.*

Pentecost was also a time of harvest, but the harvest was corn, barley, and wheat. This is the harvest mentioned in Ruth 1:22: *"So Naomi returned, and Ruth the Moabitess, her daughter in law, with her, which returned out of the country of Moab: and they came to Bethlehem in the beginning of barley harvest."* This same harvest is referenced in Ruth 2:23: *"So she kept fast by the maidens of Boaz to glean unto the end of barley harvest and of wheat harvest; and dwelt with her mother in law."* This same season is also mentioned in Exodus 34:22: *"And thou shalt observe the feast of weeks, of the firstfruits of wheat harvest, and the feast of ingathering at the year's end."*

You see, the first harvest of each year was corn, barley, and wheat, which was celebrated during the Feast of Pentecost, the time of the former rains. Corn, barley, and wheat always speak of the Word of God. The former rain refers to the preaching of the Word.

The last harvest of each year, however, was the fruit harvest, which was nourished by the latter rains and was celebrated during the Feast of Tabernacles. This speaks of the ingathering of souls and salvation of the lost.

This truth brings new meaning to James 5:7–8:

> *Be patient therefore, brethren, unto the coming of the Lord. Behold, the husbandman waiteth for the precious fruit of the earth, and hath*

*long patience for it, until he receive the early and latter rain. Be
ye also patient; stablish your hearts: for the coming of the Lord
draweth nigh.*

When the Feast of Pentecost was fulfilled prophetically during the
first century, what happened? The gospel of Christ was preached.
Thousands were added to the church daily, fulfilling the prophecies
concerning the former rains.

Now we await the coming of the latter rains and the ingathering of
all in Christ Jesus, which will take place at the end of days when the
Lord returns to rule and reign on the earth and over His ancient people,
Israel. The Bible declares: "*And so all Israel shall be saved: as it is written,
There shall come out of Sion [Zion] the Deliverer, and shall turn away ungod-
liness from Jacob: For this is my covenant unto them, when I shall take away
their sins*" (Romans 11:26–27). And in Zechariah 3:9, the Scripture tells
us, "*For behold the stone that I have laid before Joshua; upon one stone shall
be seven eyes: behold, I will engrave the graving thereof, saith the LORD of
hosts, and I will remove the iniquity of that land in one day.*"

God Almighty has promised full restitution to His people Israel.
This is the latter rain and the ingathering. So great will that ingathering be that Joel speaks of the restoration of all things, as the prophet
wrote by the Spirit, "*And I will restore to you the years that the locust hath
eaten, the cankerworm, and the caterpiller, and the palmerworm, my great
army which I sent among you*" (Joel 2:25).

This will come about as a result of the former and latter rain
coming together, for God declares, "*Be glad then, ye children of Zion, and
rejoice in the LORD your God: for he hath given you the former rain moder-
ately, and he will cause to come down for you the rain, the former rain, and
the latter rain in the first month*" (Joel 2:23).

And the prophet Amos tells us of the day when the Lord will raise
up the Tabernacle of David again, meaning this will be the time of

the full restoration of God's glory on the earth: *"In that day will I raise up the tabernacle of David that is fallen, and close up the breaches thereof; and I will raise up his ruins, and I will build it as in the days of old"* (Amos 9:11).

Through His people—Jews and Gentiles—Christ Jesus will come in glory so glorious and so great that *"the plowman shall overtake the reaper, and the treader of grapes him that soweth seed"* (Amos 9:13). This will be a time of harvest not seen since the creation of man, when *"the mountains [His government] shall drop sweet wine [His presence], and all the hills [all obstacles] shall melt"* (Amos 9:13). The presence of God will be so glorious on planet Earth that all opposition will be removed. There will not be a force on earth opposing God's presence in that day.

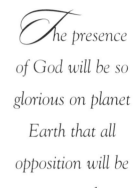

The presence of God will be so glorious on planet Earth that all opposition will be removed.

Amos continues to point to that time in verses 14–15:

> *And I will bring again the captivity of my people of Israel, and they shall build the waste cities, and inhabit them; and they shall plant vineyards, and drink the wine thereof; they shall also make gardens, and eat the fruit of them. And I will plant them upon their land, and they shall no more be pulled up out of their land which I have given them, saith the LORD thy God.*

What a glorious day that will be when we, His bride, and Israel, His chosen people, will rule and reign with our beloved Redeemer!

A FINAL WORD

The Exodus miracle is one of the most amazing accounts in all of history. The children of Israel were delivered from slavery in Egypt. They were totally healed. Even more, God gave them supernatural guidance. He *"went before them by day in a pillar of a cloud, to lead them the way; and by night in a pillar of fire, to give them light"* (Exodus 13:21). God allowed His glory to linger as they walked toward the Promised Land.

In the seven great feasts of the Lord—Passover, Unleavened Bread, Firstfruits, Pentecost, Trumpets, Day of Atonement, and Tabernacles— all point to Christ Jesus, our wonderful Lord.

Through the blood-red trail in each of the feasts, it should be apparent to all how everything in the Old Covenant pointed toward the Cross.

What was promised to the great men and women of the past has been fulfilled through Jesus Christ. He paid the price, yet we reap the reward. Oh, how precious is our Lamb of God and the faith we can have in Him.

How wonderful and true are the words that William Cowper wrote in his timeless hymn:

> There is a fountain filled with blood
> Drawn from Immanuel's veins,
> And sinners plunged beneath that flood
> Lost all their guilty stains.
>
> Dear dying Lamb, Thy precious blood
> Shall never lose its pow'r,
> Till all the ransomed Church of God
> Be saved to sin no more.

We have been ransomed by the blood of the Lamb! Jesus Christ came to earth to fulfill all the precious prophetic promises God gave throughout the Old Testament. We have the Blessed Hope, the precious Lamb of God. Best of all, He is the soon-coming King who is returning in power to receive us to live and reign with Him forever, the ransomed believers, saved to sin no more!

> And, behold, I come quickly; and my reward is with me, to give every man according as his work shall be. I am Alpha and Omega, the beginning and the end, the first and the last…. He which testifieth these things said, Surely I come quickly. Amen. Even so, come, Lord Jesus. (Revelation 22:12–13, 20)

4

TAKE UP YOUR CROSS: FOLLOW THE LAMB

Then said Jesus unto his disciples, If any man will come after me, let him deny himself, and take up his cross, and follow me.

—MATTHEW 16:24

"HE IS NO FOOL WHO GIVES what he cannot keep to gain what he cannot lose." This well-known quote by martyred missionary Jim Elliot echoes the timeless message of the Cross, plain and simple, spoken by our wonderful Master Jesus:

> *Then said Jesus unto his disciples, If any man will come after me, let him deny himself, and take up his cross, and follow me. For whosoever will save his life shall lose it: and whosoever will lose his life for my sake shall find it. For what is a man profited, if he shall gain the whole world, and lose his own soul? or what shall a man give in exchange for his soul? For the Son of man shall come in the glory of his Father with his angels; and then he shall reward every man according to his works. (Matthew 16:24–27)*

What prompts an individual to take up his cross and follow Jesus? I believe the late A. W. Tozer answered this question through his own passionate pursuit of God. He penned this profound observation in his book *The Knowledge of the Holy*, which answers this question as well:

> The yearning to know What cannot be known, to comprehend the Incomprehensible, to touch and taste the Unapproachable, arises from the image of God in the nature of man. Deep calleth unto deep, and though polluted and landlocked by the mighty disaster theologians call the Fall, the soul senses its origin and longs to return to its Source. How can this be realized? The answer of the Bible is simply "through Jesus Christ our Lord."

Throughout the pages of this book, I've shared how the Cross stands at the central point in history's time line. From the prophecies of the Old Testament to the signs and types of the Feasts, Jesus Christ is the focus of all Scripture.

Jesus Christ came to die for mankind's sins and to restore His children to a life of fellowship with the Father. Therefore, the Cross points forward, not backward. Understanding the message that we must take up our cross and follow Him is absolutely necessary to developing a walk of close fellowship with Him. It is also vital to understanding that our steps today take us ever closer to an eternity with the Savior.

The Message of the Cross

When we consider what happened at Calvary's Cross, these three things stand out:

- **The sin of mankind nailed Jesus to the cross.** All mankind was responsible for the crucifixion of our Savior. The Roman soldiers, the people watching, as well as you and I are guilty, for it was our sins—collectively and individually—that caused Him to come to earth to give Himself willingly as the ultimate sacrifice.

- **God's love is overwhelming.** It was at the Cross where both God the Father and Jesus His Son gave history's greatest gift.

- **The Savior willingly gave Himself to become mankind's only door to the Father.** *"Jesus saith unto him, I am the way, the truth, and the life: no man cometh unto the Father, but by me"* (John 14:6).

Christ was sinless, yet He became our Sin-Bearer. Instead of symbolically cleansing us from defilement and death, the Lord cleansed us from actual sin. It was through His sacrifice at Calvary that the Lord Jesus removed the ultimate obstacle, sin, that had caused centuries of estrangement between God and mankind, thereby allowing the restoration of intimate fellowship with the Father:

> *For this is good and acceptable in the sight of God our Saviour;*
> *Who will have all men to be saved, and to come unto the knowledge*
> *of the truth. For there is one God, and one mediator between God*
> *and men, the man Christ Jesus; Who gave himself a ransom for all,*
> *to be testified in due time.* (1 Timothy 2:3–6)

So, what does it mean to embrace the cross, to take it up and follow Him? What was Jesus telling us to do?

THE SECRET TO THE POWER OF THE CROSS

Let's go to the core of following Christ. I believe this is a much-needed message for God's people. The apostle Paul wrote about this need in his Holy Spirit–inspired letter to the church in Rome:

What shall we say then? Shall we continue in sin, that grace may abound? God forbid. How shall we, that are dead to sin, live any longer therein? Know ye not, that so many of us as were baptized into Jesus Christ were baptized into his death? Therefore we are buried with him by baptism into death: that like as Christ was raised up from the dead by the glory of the Father, even so we also should walk in newness of life. For if we have been planted together in the likeness of his death, we shall be also in the likeness of his resurrection: Knowing this, that our old man is crucified with him, that the body of sin might be destroyed, that henceforth we should not serve sin. For he that is dead is freed from sin. Now if we be dead with Christ, we believe that we shall also live with him: Knowing that Christ being raised from the dead dieth no more; death hath no more dominion over him. For in that he died, he died unto sin once: but in that he liveth, he liveth unto God. (Romans 6:1–10)

What we've just read has become almost foreign in the lives of too many Christians. William Barclay summed it up when he said, "The tragedy of life and of the world is not that men do not know God; the tragedy is that, knowing Him, they still insist on going their own way." We hear so little about sanctification and living the holy life. For too long, we've talked about the Christian life in terms of having a wonderful life, of finally having more meaning, of finding fulfillment and eventually going to heaven. Though these are admirable goals, they don't reflect what following Christ truly involves.

We've got to get back to the Cross. That is what the apostle Paul was expressing in a clear-cut way. And the truth, dealing with the baptism of His death, is not accepted in some circles today. Instead of preaching the Cross, they avoid the mention of it completely, preaching a Christianity that is not found in the Bible. Yet the Bible teaches death to self and the flesh, for it is the only way to victory.

Now Paul continues by telling us:

> *Likewise reckon ye also yourselves to be dead indeed unto sin, but alive unto God through Jesus Christ our Lord. Let not sin therefore reign in your mortal body, that ye should obey it in the lusts thereof. Neither yield ye your members as instruments of unrighteousness unto sin: but yield yourselves unto God, as those that are alive from the dead, and your members as instruments of righteousness unto God. For sin shall not have dominion over you: for ye are not under the law, but under grace. What then? shall we sin, because we are not under the law, but under grace? God forbid. (Romans 6:11–15)*

Reckoning yourself dead? To so many in today's world, this is unacceptable. Yet the need for dying to self has never been needed more. Self-sacrifice gives you victory over Satan. Giving your all to Jesus Christ brings abundant life, yet it starts with dying. First you must die to your self.

Jesus spoke of this in John 12:24–26, as He taught this mighty parable:

> *Verily, verily, I say unto you, Except a corn of wheat fall into the ground and die, it abideth alone: but if it die, it bringeth forth much fruit. He that loveth his life shall lose it; and he that hateth his life in this world shall keep it unto life eternal. If any man serve me, let him follow me; and where I am, there shall also my servant be: if any man serve me, him will my Father honor.*

In this parable of the wheat seed, the Lord Jesus ties serving Him and self-sacrifice together. And it was this message that God used through Kathryn Kuhlman to change my life. Attending her crusades and reading her books influenced my life in many ways. Yet it was one special tape of hers that the Holy Spirit used to totally change the way I looked at life. I was in my room and decided to listen to a tape a friend had given me, "The Secret to the Power of the Spirit." I hadn't been a Christian very long, and my friend told me that this tape was something I really must listen to. I put the tape in the machine, and the moment it began to play, the power of God came on me, and I was instantly riveted to every word.

As the message continued, she began talking about dying to self. She told how before she would walk onto the platform, she died a thousand deaths. At first I didn't really understand all she was saying, but I kept listening because I felt such a presence of the Holy Spirit. I kept rewinding the tape and listening to the words over and over until I finally began to understand what this wonderful woman of God was saying.

The decision to die to yourself must be made continually. We must reckon ourselves dead.

"The secret to the power of the Holy Spirit," she said, "is dependence upon Him, not independence."

She went on to describe how she had finally yielded to Him completely —body, spirit, and soul—one Saturday in Los Angeles at four o'clock in the afternoon. She said that the experience caused a transformation in her life.

That was a turning point for me as the truth of her message began to transform my life. I realized that it wasn't just one transformation, but it was a constant revelation of dying to self. None of us, except our wonderful Master Jesus, has ever lived a perfect life. The decision to die to yourself must be made continually. We must reckon ourselves dead. And once we bury self, we must allow God to bring forth the new man that He desires. We must allow Him to develop the image of His Son in us on a daily basis.

It all starts with dying to your self. It continues when you die daily. Following Christ means embracing the Cross every day.

Total Dependence

What does it mean to be totally dependent upon the Savior? Let me go back to the Old Testament for an undeniable example. King David, considered by historians and scholars to be one of the most powerful and successful warriors of his day, was very willing to openly declare that without God he could do nothing. This thought runs throughout the longest chapter in the Bible. When I saw what the psalmist was saying, I began seeing the entire passage of Psalm 119 as an insightful discourse of total dependence upon God, based on a foundation of obedience and cleanliness.

He starts the psalm by declaring: *"Blessed are the undefiled in the way, who walk in the law of the LORD. Blessed are they that keep his testimonies, and that seek him with the whole heart. They also do no iniquity: they walk in his ways"* (verses 1–3), clearly telling us that we cannot live a holy life without total dependence upon God.

Now, notice David's dependence upon the Lord in the following passages from Psalm 119 (emphasis mine):

> *Thou hast commanded us to keep thy precepts diligently.* **O that my ways were directed to keep thy statutes!** *Then shall I not be ashamed, when I have respect unto all thy commandments. I will keep thy statutes:* **O forsake me not utterly.** (verses 4–6, 8)

> *Wherewithal shall a young man cleanse his way?* **by taking heed thereto according to thy word.** (verse 9)

With my whole heart have I sought thee: **O let me not wander from thy commandments.** *Thy word have I hid in mine heart, that I might not sin against thee. Blessed art thou, O* LORD: **teach me thy statutes.** (verses 10–12)

Open thou mine eyes, *that I may behold wondrous things out of thy law. I am a stranger in the earth:* **hide not thy commandments from me.** (verses 18–19)

Thou hast rebuked the proud that are cursed, which do err from thy commandments. **Remove from me reproach and contempt;** *for I have kept thy testimonies.* (verses 21–22)

My soul cleaveth unto the dust: **quicken thou me according to thy word.** *I have declared my ways, and thou heardest me:* **teach me thy statutes. Make me to understand the way of thy precepts:** *so shall I talk of thy wondrous works.* (verses 25–27)

Teach me, O LORD, **the way of thy statutes;** *and I shall keep it unto the end.* **Give me understanding,** *and I shall keep thy law; yea, I shall observe it with my whole heart.* (verses 33–34)

Stablish thy word unto thy servant, *who is devoted to thy fear.* (verse 38)

Let my heart be sound in thy statutes; *that I be not ashamed. My soul fainteth for thy salvation: but* **I hope in thy word.** (verses 80–81)

Uphold me according unto thy word, *that I may live: and* **let me not be ashamed of my hope. Hold thou me up,** *and I shall be safe: and I will have respect unto thy statutes continually.* (verses 116–117)

The entrance of thy words giveth light; it giveth understanding unto the simple. I opened my mouth, and panted: for I longed for thy commandments. **Look thou upon me, and be merciful unto me,** *as thou usest to do unto those that love thy name.* **Order my steps in thy word: and let not any iniquity have dominion over me.** (verses 130–133)

King David concludes Psalm 119 with a remorseful sense of his own sin and overwhelming dependence upon God's grace:

Let thine hand help me; for I have chosen thy precepts. I have longed for thy salvation, O Lord; and thy law is my delight. **Let my soul live,** *and it shall praise thee; and* **let thy judgments help me. I have gone astray like a lost sheep; seek thy servant;** *for I do not forget thy commandments.* (verses 173–176)

In this last verse David shows his total dependence upon the Lord by asking God to seek His servant. This utter dependence is only possible through the power of the Holy Spirit's insight and help. When it comes to seeking Him, it is vital to remember that He sought us first. The Word of God tells us how deeply God loves us and desires for us to be in close fellowship with Him.

Oh, that we would pray daily, "Lord Jesus, I am dependent upon You and the work You did on the cross. Help me. I rely completely upon You today for wisdom, strength, and revelation so I can serve You better today."

Back to the Cross

Why does dying to self seem so foreign and so difficult to so many? It is because every satanic force in the universe is dedicated to keeping men and women from the Cross. And should that be a surprise? After all, the devil hates the Cross. The second you and I yield to the Cross and offer our own life as a sacrifice to the Lord Jesus, the Son of God, it is then that Satan's power is destroyed.

Throughout history, the Cross has been God's weapon against the enemy.

- When the children of Israel were ready to leave Egypt, God revealed the Cross (door post and lintels) and protected Israel from the angel of death (Exodus 12).

- After they left Egypt and came to Marah, God revealed the Cross (the tree) and then gave the covenant of healing (Exodus 15).

- Then when serpents bit the people as a result of sin, and as the death toll grew, again God revealed the Cross (the pole), delivering His own children (Numbers 21).

- After David numbered the people and a plague killed thousands of Israelites, God again revealed the Cross (the wood from the threshing instruments) in the blood sacrifice and offerings made to the Lord, causing the plague to stop (2 Samuel 24).

So Paul declares, *"But God forbid that I should glory, save in the cross of our Lord Jesus Christ"* (Galatians 6:14).

The enemy will do anything, anything, to keep you from the cross, from dying to self, from sacrificing your will. The apostle Paul knew this well when he wrote, *"I am crucified with Christ: nevertheless I live; yet not I, but Christ liveth in me: and the life which I now live in the flesh I live by the faith of the Son of God, who loved me, and gave himself for me"* (Galatians 2:20).

A Final Word

The first thing God asks of any believer is to offer himself or herself up as a sacrifice. And even when you say, "Yes, Lord, I will die to myself," the battle is just beginning. Sanctification, which means "increasing participation in His death," signifies that we voluntarily offer our life on the cross and throw ourselves in full dependence upon the Lord.

It took Abraham nearly a hundred years to sacrifice himself on the altar of God's perfect will.

It took Moses eighty years to reach the point where he was able to set himself aside in order for God the Father to use him to free an entire nation from slavery and death.

It took the apostle Paul fourteen or more years to reach this point after being struck down by a blinding light on the road to Damascus. He had to go to the desert of Arabia to seek God's face. He had to go through torture and disappointment. Eventually he was able to say, "I am crucified with Christ." The Holy Spirit used Paul's "reckoning" to touch the known world. The reverberations from his "not me, but Christ who lives in me" continue to this day.

Every man or woman who has been used mightily of God to reach others with the gospel of Jesus Christ has similar sounding testimonies of learning how to crucify themselves without regard to self-preservation or self-worth.

And it was after Kathryn Kuhlman experienced death to self and discovered the meaning of "No longer I, but Christ," that the Lord was able to shake the world through her evangelistic and healing ministry.

Jesus said, *"He that loveth his life shall lose it; and he that hateth his life in this world shall keep it unto life eternal"* (John 12:25). How do you hate your life? You die daily. You sacrifice all to Him.

You say you want abundant life? You say you want to be victorious? You can't wait to be used of God? Consider the passage inspired by the Holy Spirit and penned by the apostle Paul to the church in Rome. In the midst of wonderful, eternal promises, the command is once again given for believers to die daily:

> *What shall we then say to these things? If God be for us, who can be against us? He that spared not his own Son, but delivered him up for us all, how shall he not with him also freely give us all things? Who shall lay any thing to the charge of God's elect? It is God that justifieth. Who is he that condemneth? It is Christ that died, yea rather, that is risen again, who is even at the right hand of God, who also maketh intercession for us. Who shall separate us from the love of Christ? shall tribulation, or distress, or persecution, or famine, or nakedness, or peril, or sword? As it is written, For thy sake we are killed all the day long; we are accounted as sheep for the slaughter. Nay, in all these things we are more than conquerors through him that loved us. For I am persuaded, that neither death, nor life, nor angels, nor principalities, nor powers, nor things present, nor things to come, nor height, nor depth, nor any other creature, shall be able to separate us from the love of God, which is in Christ Jesus our Lord. (Romans 8:31–39)*

Are you willing to nail your self, your life, and your desires to the Cross? The words to the invitation hymn are clear and direct:

> I surrender all.
> I surrender all.
> All to Thee, my blessed Savior,
> I surrender all.

Jesus paid the price on the cross of Calvary for you to live victoriously; but before you can live, you must die to self and the things of the world. Today, Jesus says, "Follow me." That path goes to the Cross. He offers the power to shake your world with the life-changing and miracle-working gospel. Only death to self will access this kind of power.

Satan wants you to live a crossless life, which advertises adventure and happiness, yet leads to an empty, pointless existence, and death. Jesus offers the Cross-filled life, which begins with death to self, then leads to abundance, glorious living, and victory in every area of your life, plus an eternity with the Father.

The choices we make, taking up our cross and following Him, will make the difference for all eternity.

Jesus offers the Cross-filled life, which begins with death to self, then leads to abundance, glorious living, and victory in every area of your life.

5

REDEMPTION BY THE LAMB: 7 ETERNAL BLESSINGS

And they sung a new song, saying, Thou art worthy to take the book, and to open the seals thereof: for thou wast slain, and hast redeemed us to God by thy blood out of every kindred, and tongue, and people, and nation; And hast made us unto our God kings and priests: and we shall reign on the earth.

—REVELATION 5:9–10

YOU HAVE BEEN BOUGHT AND PURCHASED. The blood of the Lamb was shed to redeem you. Yet what does it mean to be redeemed?

- It means you are no longer the devil's possession. Jesus Christ came and purchased you with His own life and blood.

- It also means you are God's possession. That means every part of you belongs to heaven, and all you have to do is to accept Jesus as Savior to be redeemed with His ultimate price.

Since that is the case, you can choose to walk like you are redeemed, talk like it, and look like it. You are not Satan's; you are God's child. You don't belong to the world; you belong to heaven.

Since heaven has already chosen you, it's up to you now to choose heaven. You are redeemed by the blood of the Lamb! You can join the psalmist in saying: "*O give thanks unto the LORD, for he is good: for his mercy endureth for ever. Let the redeemed of the LORD say so, whom he hath redeemed from the hand of the enemy*" (Psalm 107:1–2).

And as you read Ephesians 1, the entire plan for your redemption and salvation is revealed:

> *Just as He chose us in Him before the foundation of the world, that we should be holy and without blame before Him in love, having predestined us to adoption as sons by Jesus Christ to Himself, according to the good pleasure of His will, to the praise of the glory of His grace, by which He has made us accepted in the Beloved. In Him we have redemption through His blood, the forgiveness of sins, according to the riches of His grace.* (1:4–7, NKJV)

MANKIND'S NEED

God created man in His own image (Genesis 1:27), formed him "*of the dust of the ground, and breathed into his nostrils the breath of life; and man became a living soul*" (Genesis 2:7). God gave him the earth to subdue and oversee. Adam ruled and reigned with God on planet Earth. All man's needs were met, and he enjoyed rich fellowship and communion with God. However, the enemy of mankind's soul, Satan, "*more subtle than any beast of the field*" (Genesis 3:1), deceived Eve. Adam soon joined her in this deception as they both disobeyed God's command: "*Of the tree of the knowledge of good and evil, thou shalt not eat of it: for in the day that thou eatest thereof thou shalt surely die*" (Genesis 2:17). Their disobedience brought severe conse- quences—spiritual death, bondage to Satan, and eternal separation from God.

In the words of the late A. W. Tozer, a noted writer and one of my personal heroes of the faith:

> What a tragedy! Created to be a mirror to the Almighty, Adam and Eve forfeited the glory of God. Made in God's image, Adam and Eve were more like Him than the angels above. God had created man so He could look into him and see reflected there more of His own glory than He could see reflected in the starry skies above.

When Adam sinned against God, he violated the loving relationship that had existed. From that moment until Christ died on Calvary's cross, man was held captive by Satan's power.

As shared in the early chapters of this book, Old Testament prophets looked toward the day when they would be liberated from sin's curse. And because God is not willing that anyone should perish eternally (2 Peter 3:9), He took the first step toward reconciliation. By sending His Son as the sinless sacrifice and substitute for mankind, God offered a way in which man could be redeemed and reconciled back to Him through His Son, Jesus Christ.

God's Perfect Timing

God sent His Son to die for humanity. Even though it was man who turned his back on the relationship he had enjoyed with God, because of God's perfect love toward man, the Father took the first step toward redeeming and reconciling mankind back to a right relationship with Him by sending His Son to die for you and me:

> *But God commendeth his love toward us, in that, while we were yet sinners, Christ died for us. Much more then, being now justified by his*

blood, we shall be saved from wrath through him. For if, when we were enemies, we were reconciled to God by the death of his Son, much more, being reconciled, we shall be saved by his life. (Romans 8:10–12)

Jesus willingly became our substitute, giving His life on the cross of Calvary and shedding His blood to atone for sin. The price He paid made it possible for all mankind to be free from the penalty of sin, eternal separation from God. Through Jesus Christ and His shed blood, we are forgiven, cleansed, redeemed, and justified: *"In whom we have redemption through his blood, the forgiveness of sins, according to the riches of his grace"* (Ephesians 1:7).

Because of God's grace, our sin is not only pardoned, it is put away forever as if it had never existed. We are pronounced innocent of all guilt. This wonderful gift is the result of God's perfect love and grace toward man, allowing man to be viewed as innocent and reconciled to God, to enjoy a relationship with our Father, as Adam and Eve knew in the Garden of Eden.

He Purchased All of You

Dr. Winston Nunes was a wonderful Canadian Bible scholar who sowed a great deal into my life when I was a young man. He was a dear man of God who, until he went to heaven in 1999, committed his life to helping others understand God's Word and God's ways. He made this startling statement: "God Almighty is not going from here to redemption; he's going from redemption to there."

God begins from redemption on. He's not bringing us to the place of redemption. He begins with redemption. Dr. Nunes went on to say, "The fact is, we are redeemed already."

When you know you're redeemed, your walk with God will change.

You'll see yourself in a new light. You'll see yourself in a different way. When you know you are redeemed, you know Satan cannot touch you or your mind or your body or any part of you. Why? Because you are redeemed!

Do you really understand what it means to be purchased? It means Christ Jesus has complete authority and rights over you. It means no foreign power can touch your life. When you are purchased, it means Satan and all his hosts have no right to touch you.

The devil's success is dependent upon our ignorance. When you don't know who you are, then he comes and touches you, trying to ruin you. He comes and strikes at you. You must stand strong in Christ and know who you are in Him. You are redeemed! You are purchased! You are His!

Every part of you is His. You are bone of His bones and flesh of His flesh. Not only is your heart His, your soul is His and your body is His. The Word of God says the body is for the Lord. When you stand in the knowledge that even every hair on your head is His (that is why He numbered them, as explained by Jesus in Matthew 10:30), you will not tolerate any foreign power touching you, for you belong to God Almighty.

Every part of you is His. You are bone of His bones and flesh of His flesh. Not only is your heart His, your soul is His and your body is His.

God has placed such incredible value on you that the blood of his Son paid for you. Think about sacrificing your own child to pay for someone else's sin. Could you do it? No, in our human strength we could not. Nevertheless, God did! God Almighty gave His only begotten Son, and saw Him slain on a cross to buy back sinners. Jesus died for the rotten, the filthy, the bound, the oppressed, and the demon possessed.

The price has been paid for every man, every woman, every boy, every girl. And all you have to do is say yes. The book of Isaiah declares: *"But now thus saith the LORD that created thee, O Jacob, and he that formed thee, O Israel, fear not: for I have redeemed thee, I have called thee by thy name; thou art mine"* (Isaiah 43:1).

We surrender to Him because we are not our own. When you hold back, you sin against Him. When you hold back, you say to God: "God, You can't have me; I am my own person."

Remember Paul's message? You are not your own. You don't belong even to yourself. You belong to Jesus. The price is paid. The purchase is complete. The redemption is done. For you to hold back is to hold back on His grace, mercy, and power in your life.

I was in prayer recently about a challenge I had struggled with for several months. There are many responsibilities connected with running a worldwide ministry, and though I won't belabor you with the specific challenge, it was something that I couldn't seem to solve. The Lord spoke to me as I was praying and said, "Don't you realize you are Mine?"

I said, "Lord, I know that."

He said, "If you are Mine, so are your problems." He said, "Why do you give Me your body, but not your problems?"

I said, "Lord, I didn't think You wanted my problems."

He said, "I purchased not only you, but your problems, too."

He definitely won that exchange, for which I remain very grateful. His ways are always better than our ways. Why not cast our cares upon Him?

WHY HOLD BACK?

We are redeemed, yet how often we fail to cast all our cares and problems on the Lord. Perhaps they seem too dirty, too problematic, too confusing, or even too embarrassing. We say, "Oh, Jesus, I give you my soul, my body, my life, but I can't give you this." The Word of God admonishes, *"Cast thy burden upon the LORD, and he shall sustain thee: he shall never suffer the righteous to be moved"* (Psalm 55:22).

I love to read books written by the wonderful writers of the past. The works of R. A. Torrey have affected my life greatly. On this subject he said, "We sometimes fear to bring our troubles to God, because they must seem small to Him who sitteth on the circle of the earth. But if they are large enough to vex and endanger our welfare, they are large enough to touch His heart of love. For love does not measure by a merchant's scales, nor with a surveyor's chain. It hath a delicacy...unknown in any material substance."

God is concerned about every area of a believer's life. We should hold nothing back from Him. Everything is His. You are bought with a price, not only you, but everything you own, everything you have. That includes all of your troubles, joys, sorrows, difficulties, pluses, and minuses. Everything is His! We no longer own them. The problem is that too often we try to regain possession of all those familiar things that hold us back from serving Him wholeheartedly.

There was a man in Russia many years ago, during the Soviet tyranny who had been put in a pit while in prison. He had not seen a human face in ages. They fed him by pushing food under the door. It was dark; he had not seen the sunlight in months. He was in one of the worst situations you can be in. For a long time he had not heard a human voice. Until one day, Jesus appeared to him. He was so over-whelmed and so moved that Jesus Christ would visit him! He said, "Oh, dear Jesus, what can I give You back in return just to say thank You?"

The Lord told him, "All is Mine."

The man said again, "There must be something I can give You back to say thank You that You would come to visit me."

The Lord said again, "All is Mine; there's nothing you can give Me."

Yet again the man cried, "Oh Lord, there must be something I can give You."

The Lord replied, "Give Me your sin."

The man said, "There surely must be something better I can give You."

Jesus said, "No, even your sin is Mine."

Think about that. He purchased not only you, but also your sin. What a Lord we serve! Not only can we give Him our body, but also our sin!

It reminds me of a powerful scene from a 1955 movie called *A Man Called Peter.* This is the well-told, tender, Academy Award–nominated story of Peter Marshall, a Scottish minister who traveled to America and eventually pastored the Church of Presidents in our nation's capital. He also served as chaplain in the United States Senate. I remember one particular scene in which Catherine Marshall, his wife, was sick. She prayed, yet nothing happened. No healing came her way. Finally she yielded to the will of God. God healed her the moment she surrendered everything to Him.

How often we may say, "Heal me! Heal me! Heal me!" Yet nothing happens. Instead, we need to give Christ our sickness. Do you realize nothing belongs to you, not even your soul? So, why are you holding on to the things that keep you from moving forward in faith?

Let the Redeemed of the Lord Say So!

You have been redeemed from all iniquity. No sin can dominate your life because you are purchased. As Christians, we are set apart as a peculiar people, zealous of good works:

> *Looking for that blessed hope, and the glorious appearing of the great God and our Saviour Jesus Christ; Who gave himself for us, that he might redeem us from all iniquity, and purify unto himself a peculiar people, zealous of good works.* (Titus 2:13–14)

And so God has taken you out of the hand of the Enemy: *"And I will deliver thee out of the hand of the wicked, and I will redeem thee out of the hand of the terrible"* (Jeremiah 15:21). Satan cannot have you, nor can he touch you. The Bible gives us these mighty promises, yet it is up to us as believers to live in it, walk in it, and fill our lives with God's Word.

Even death cannot take hold of you. God says: *"I will ransom them from the power of the grave; I will redeem them from death"* (Hosea 13:14). Death does not own you; life owns you! You must allow this to sink deep in your spirit and speak it forth from your lips. Psalm 107:2 declares: *"Let the redeemed of the LORD say so, whom he hath redeemed from the hand of the enemy."*

It's time to say so. Why should you speak out loud of your redemption? It's time to claim all that the Lamb of God has provided for you through the Cross of Calvary. It's to remind the devil of his defeat. In fact, every time you say, "I'm redeemed!" the devil remembers his loss.

Because You Are Redeemed by the Lamb of God

Once you accept Jesus Christ into your heart, asking Him to be your Savior and the Lord of your life, great authority is available to you as you learn to appropriate the power of the blood covenant. You are able to experience victory today because of the His blood. There are many wonderful promises in God's Word dealing with the blood. Here are seven blessings we receive through redemption by the blood of the Lamb.

1. Because you are redeemed by the Lamb, the Holy Spirit is yours.

The Holy Spirit was given to us because of redemption and the Cross. Peter tells us this in 1 Peter 1:2: *"Elect according to the foreknowledge of God the Father, through sanctification of the Spirit, unto obedience and sprinkling of* the blood of Jesus Christ: *Grace unto you, and peace, be multiplied.*" The redemptive work of Christ gives us the Holy Spirit.

And the Holy Ghost answers to the blood. The blood always brought the fire down in the Old Covenant, and so it is today: the blood brings the Spirit of the Lord upon your life. The Bible says that the Holy Ghost and the blood agree: "*And there are three that bear witness in earth, the spirit, and the water, and the blood: and these three agree in one*" (1 John 5:8).

> *You'll never find the presence of the Holy Ghost without the blood availing, touching, cleansing, and purifying.*

The Holy Ghost is upon you because you are redeemed. The Holy Spirit and the blood of the Lamb are in total agreement. Where the blood is, the Holy Ghost is. Where the Holy Ghost is, the blood is. You'll never find the presence of the Holy Ghost without the blood availing, touching, cleansing, and purifying.

Wherever you see the sprinkling of the blood, you'll see the Holy Ghost active, moving, and touching lives.

2. **Because you are redeemed by the Lamb, you are reconciled to God.**

Paul's Holy Spirit–inspired letter to the Colossian church shares another promise of the blood of the Lamb: "*And, having made peace through the blood of his cross, by him to reconcile all things unto himself; by him, I say, whether they be things in earth, or things in heaven*" (Colossians 1:20).

The blood redeems you, and once you are redeemed you are reconciled to God. The power of the blood of Christ removes all that separates you and me from God. It restores our relationship and our fellowship with God. In reconciliation, the Holy Ghost is yours, and the presence of God is yours in its entirety.

Do you know that when Jesus bought you and made you His own, His presence became yours eternally?

3. Because you are redeemed by the Lamb, you are continually cleansed.

Because of the blood of the Lamb, we receive cleansing in Christ. There is an uninterrupted abiding in Him through the cleansing of the blood. Scripture declares: *"But if we walk in the light, as he is in the light, we have fellowship one with another, and the blood of Jesus Christ his Son cleanseth us from all sin"* (1 John 1:7).

Cleanseth. That's present tense.

How do you walk in the light so you can receive such wonderful cleansing? You simply confess your sin to Him and receive His forgiveness. When we do, according to Scripture, He's faithful and just to forgive us our sin and to cleanse us from all unrighteousness. There is an uninterrupted flow of cleansing power in Christ Jesus. His blood has abiding power that keeps cleaning us continually.

Cleansing does not come to you once a week or even every day. It comes in Christ every second. The blood has abiding cleansing power because you have been purchased. I love what Revelation 1:5–6 says:

> *And from Jesus Christ, who is the faithful witness, and the first begotten of the dead, and the prince of the kings of the earth. Unto him that loved us, and washed us from our sins in his own blood, and hath made us kings and priests unto God and his Father; to him be glory and dominion for ever and ever. Amen.*

When God looks at you, He sees no sin. He sees the blood of Christ cleansing you. You are cleansed, wholly and completely clean. The blood of the Lamb makes you pure in the sight of God. It's as if you have never sinned. Hallelujah!

4. Because you are redeemed by the Lamb, you are sanctified.

Hebrews 13:12 says: *"Wherefore Jesus also, that he might sanctify the people with his own blood, suffered without the gate."*

And when you are sanctified, you become a vessel of honor set apart for the Master's use. The apostle Paul, writing under the inspiration of the Holy Spirit, gave this clear-cut description in 2 Timothy 2:21: *"If a man therefore purge himself from these, he shall be a vessel unto honor, sanctified, and meet for the master's use, and prepared unto every good work."*

God chose you and set you apart because He loves you. There is a most remarkable portion of Scripture in Deuteronomy which attests to this truth:

> For thou art a holy people unto the LORD thy God: the LORD thy God hath chosen thee to be a special people unto himself, above all people that are upon the face of the earth. The LORD did not set his love upon you, nor choose you, because ye were more in number than any people; for ye were the fewest of all people: But because the LORD loved you, and because he would keep the oath which he had sworn unto your fathers, hath the LORD brought you out with a mighty hand, and redeemed you out of the house of bondmen, from the hand of Pharaoh king of Egypt. (7:6–8)

The Holy Ghost is yours, the presence of God is yours, continual cleansing is yours, and sanctification belongs to you when you are washed in the blood of Christ.

5. Because you are redeemed by the Lamb, you are perfected.

Hebrews 10:14 tells us an important truth: *"For by one offering he hath perfected for ever them that are sanctified."* And having perfected us, He does not remember our sins, nor bring them to our remembrance.

Think about the fact that God says He will not remember your sins anymore. Can you picture the day when you will stand before Jesus in glory? He will not remind you of your sins, because every sin is forgotten. Every sin is under the blood. Every sin has been washed away. You are perfect. Now that's a staggering statement, yet it is the Word of God!

6. Because you are redeemed by the Lamb, you pass from death to life.

The moment you receive Jesus in your life, you pass from sin to righteousness and from darkness to life through His blood:

> *Verily, verily, I say unto you, He that heareth my word, and believeth on him that sent me, hath everlasting life, and shall not come into condemnation; but is passed from death unto life.* (John 5:24)

> *To open their eyes, and to turn them from darkness to light, and from the power of Satan unto God, that they may receive forgiveness of sins, and inheritance among them which are sanctified by faith that is in me.* (Acts 26:18)

> *But God commendeth his love toward us, in that, while we were yet sinners, Christ died for us. Much more then, being now justified by his blood, we shall be saved from wrath through him. For if, when we were enemies, we were reconciled to God by the death of his Son,*

much more, being reconciled, we shall be saved by his life. (Romans 5:8–10)

Giving thanks unto the Father, which hath made us meet to be partakers of the inheritance of the saints in light: Who hath delivered us from the power of darkness, and hath translated us into the kingdom of his dear Son: In whom we have redemption through his blood, even the forgiveness of sins. (Colossians 1:12–14)

The blood of Christ causes judgment to pass over your life as you are delivered from Satan's domain. Likewise, as the blood of a lamb was applied to the house of the Israelites no plague came upon them or destroyed them: "*And the blood shall be to you for a token upon the houses where ye are: and when I see the blood, I will pass over you, and the plague shall not be upon you to destroy you, when I smite the land of Egypt*" (Exodus 12:13).

Judgment only falls upon those living in the world. Grace covers the lives of those who have received Christ Jesus because of His precious blood that was shed.

7. Because you are redeemed by the Lamb, you can come boldly before God's throne.

Not only are you perfected in Christ, you have also been given boldness to enter God's holy presence.

Having therefore, brethren, boldness to enter into the holiest by the blood of Jesus, by a new and living way, which he hath consecrated for us, through the veil, that is to say, his flesh; And having an high priest over the house of God; Let us draw near with a true heart in full assurance of faith, having our hearts sprinkled from an evil

conscience, and our bodies washed with pure water. Let us hold fast
the profession of our faith without wavering; (for he is faithful that
promised.) (Hebrews 10:19–23)

Always remember, every promise in the Bible belongs to you.
That's why the Word says He's *"faithful that promised."* You can walk in
and claim every promise in the Bible. You can walk into the presence
of God today because you are bought with the blood of the Lamb.

Remember the story of Esther? It's an exciting account that believers should read often. Mordecai said to Esther, "You better go in and
ask for your life and the lives of your people."

Esther responded, "Look, if I should walk in uninvited, I'd be slain."
The law of the Medes and the Persians in that day was such that if the
king did not call for you, you would die trying to get in.

I have news for you today! The King has called for you! Every day
He says, "Come on in."

You are bought, you are purchased, and you are redeemed. You
belong to God! You don't have to enter His presence fearing for your
own life as they did in Esther's day. All you must do is to come in and
make your requests known, through a new and living way, which is the
blood of Jesus Christ.

> *Verily, verily, I say unto you, He that believeth on me, the works*
> *that I do shall he do also; and greater works than these shall he do;*
> *because I go unto my Father. And whatsoever ye shall ask in my*
> *name, that will I do, that the Father may be glorified in the Son.*
> (John 14:12-13)

Once you are in His presence, you can ask for whatever you will as
He makes His will known to you. He'll give it to you. Why? Because
He said "verily, verily," which means "truthfully, truthfully." What a

wonderful promise which becomes available to you when you accept the Lamb of God into your heart and life!

A Final Word

There are so many promises that come your way when your heart is washed with the blood of the Lamb. The Bible is filled with them; so much, in fact, that it could take the rest of your life to explore all of them.

For instance, the book of Revelation contains a mighty promise of God for you today: "*And they overcame him by the blood of the Lamb, and by the word of their testimony; and they loved not their lives unto the death*" (12:11).

In Christ, you have victory and protection. Just as the blood of a lamb brought Passover for the Israelites, so with the blood of Christ Jesus, the Lamb of God is your Passover. No evil can come to you because of the blood; evil must pass over.

> *For the* LORD *will pass through to smite the Egyptians; and when he seeth the blood upon the lintel, and on the two side posts, the* LORD *will pass over the door, and will not suffer the destroyer to come in unto your houses to smite you.* (Exodus 12:23)

In prayer, you can apply His blood to your life, your families' lives, to your home and your possessions. In Exodus, the children of Israel applied the blood of a lamb to their door posts. Later, Moses sprinkled the blood on every piece of furniture in the tabernacle. He applied the blood on the books and on the people. (See Hebrews 9:19–21). Likewise, you can also cover your home with the blood of Christ. You are not only bought through the work of the Savior on the cross, you are covered with His blood.

Now, more than ever, you can sing the wonderful Fanny Crosby song:

> Redeemed, how I love to proclaim it!
> Redeemed by the blood of the Lamb;
> Redeemed through His infinite mercy,
> His child and forever I am.
>
> I think of my blessed Redeemer,
> I think of Him all the day long:
> I sing, for I cannot be silent;
> His love is the theme of my song.
>
> Redeemed, redeemed,
> Redeemed by the blood of the Lamb;
> Redeemed, redeemed,
> His child and forever I am.

Let the redeemed of the Lord say so! The Lord has defeated every enemy. Victory is yours today! You are redeemed. What an exciting life filled with expectation of all His blessings when we receive redemption through the blood of the Lamb of God!

The Lamb of God and You

The Lord is my helper, and I will not fear what man shall do unto me…. Jesus Christ the same yesterday, and to day, and for ever.

—Hebrews 13: 6, 8

H<small>E WAS BORN IN BETHLEHEM</small> to a virgin, miraculously conceived through the Holy Spirit, and lived a sinless life in the small, dusty village of Nazareth. Until He began His public ministry at the age of thirty, Jesus worked as a carpenter. For three years, He traveled with a small group of followers, never journeying more than a few hundred miles from His birthplace, usually on foot or by boat.

History reveals that the Son of Man did not own major buildings or launch vast entrepreneurial enterprises. He didn't have any ecclesiastical titles or hold noteworthy political positions. He earned no diplomas or academic credentials from the leading scholastic centers of His time, and He never penned a book.

Even after spending so much time with the twelve disciples, and sharing such powerful, intimate moments as they sat and learned at His feet, His closest friends abandoned and even betrayed Him when His enemies sought to kill Him. He was mocked on trial and in public as a delusional madman. Naked and bleeding, He was nailed in full view of gawking spectators on Golgotha's hill, left to die in shame between two common thieves. When He was pronounced dead, He was buried in someone else's grave with no fanfare.

Yet today, He remains the centerpiece of history. More than twenty centuries have passed, and still He remains the most powerful force known to mankind. Massive armies have come and gone, powerful political systems have risen and fallen, all-powerful dictators and kings have crumbled to dust—yet all of them combined have never impacted the world as did this Son of Man named Jesus Christ the Savior. He is, after all, *"Jesus Christ the same yesterday, and to day, and for ever"* (Hebrews 13:8). He continues to change hearts and lives today. And because He died on the cross in shame, the Word of God declares that one day every knee will bow and every tongue will confess that He is Lord.

> *Christ Jesus, who, being in the form of God, did not consider it robbery to be equal with God, but made Himself of no reputation, taking the form of a bondservant, and coming in the likeness of men. And being found in appearance as a man, He humbled Himself and became obedient to the point of death, even the death of the cross. Therefore God also has highly exalted Him and given Him the name which is above every name, that at the name of Jesus every knee should bow, of those in heaven, and of those on earth, and of those under the earth, and that every tongue should confess that Jesus Christ is Lord, to the glory of God the Father.* (Philippians 2:5–11, NKJV)

A PERSONAL INVITATION

Anytime I communicate with people through books, crusades, broadcasts, or talking one-on-one, I'm aware that people come from a variety of backgrounds. Perhaps you have been a dedicated Christian for many years. Others, perhaps you, have never heard or understood the gospel before and are desperately seeking answers for questions you thought you'd never be asking. If the next few paragraphs don't relate to you, please realize that other readers are starting from different places and perspectives.

Still, here is a basic starting point for everyone: Regardless of your background, education, or culture, the first step toward a life of forgiveness and an eternity in heaven is making sure you have Jesus living in your heart.

No matter what situation or set of challenges you face at this exact moment, God wants to give you the answers to all the questions you face. He gave His own Son to offer freedom from guilt and a peace that the world cannot give. The Creator of the universe offered Jesus Christ as the *"Lamb of God, which taketh away the sin of the world"* (John 1:29) so He could draw each of us to Himself. That's how much He cared, still cares, and will care for you and me. We do not have to feel alienated or separated from Him. He wants to be in close fellowship with us.

It is a historical fact that He died on the cross and rose from the grave. By those supernatural acts, Jesus Christ paid the penalty for our sin and rebellion against God. He, alone, bridges the gap between God and man. John 3:16, in fact, states: *"For God so loved the world, that he gave his only begotten Son, that whosoever believeth in him should not perish, but have everlasting life."*

You can have a close, eternal relationship with Him by trusting in Christ Jesus alone to save you from the curse that has fallen on all mankind. In fact, when you confess your sins and receive Him into your heart, God gives you the right to become His forgiven child: *"But as many as received him, to them he gave the power to become the sons of God, even to them who believe on his name"* (John 1:12).

It really is that simple. I am living proof. My life began changing from the time I knelt as a teenager and asked the Savior to come into my heart. My family members, one by one, came to the same knowledge as they accepted the Savior. Since then, I've seen the most skeptical hearts touched and impossibly desperate lives changed all over the world.

Dear reader, if you haven't done so already, is there any good reason why you cannot receive Jesus Christ into your heart right now? If you are willing to let go of your burdens and sin and if you will repent and receive Jesus Christ as your Lord and Savior, you can do it right now. At this moment you can pray the most important prayer of your life. You can use words such as these:

Dear Lord Jesus, I believe You are the Son of God. I believe You came to earth 2,000 years ago. I believe You died for me on the cross and shed Your blood for my salvation. I believe You rose from the dead and ascended on high. I believe You are coming back again to earth. Dear Jesus, I am a sinner. Forgive my sin; cleanse me now with Your precious blood. Come into my heart, save my soul. Right now I surrender, the best I know how. I give You my life. I proclaim You the Lord of my life, my Savior, my God. Today, I declare I no longer belong to Satan; I belong to Jesus. God Almighty is my heavenly Father; Jesus Christ, my Savior; the Holy Spirit, my Comforter. And I proclaim that I am Yours forever, washed in Your blood, and I am born again. Amen.

If you prayed that prayer and meant it, the Bible has more life-changing promises for you, including the one found in Romans 10:13: *"For whoever shall call upon the name of the Lord shall be saved."*

The Bible also tells us: *"Therefore if any man be in Christ, he is a new creature: old things are passed away; behold, all things are become new"* (2 Corinthians 5:17).

The Scriptures declare: *"In whom we have redemption through his blood, the forgiveness of sins, according to the riches of his grace"* (Ephesians 1:7). This redemption is what the apostle Paul pointed to when he wrote: *"For ye are bought with a price: therefore glorify God in your body, and in your spirit, which are God's"* (1 Corinthians 6:20).

Receive Jesus. Embrace Christ. Love the Lamb of God. Surrender to the Savior. Look for His soon return as you serve Him faithfully. Plan to spend eternity with Him around the throne of God because of the work He did at Calvary.

A Final Note

If you have received Jesus into your heart while reading this book, please let me know. You can call 817-722-2222 or go online to www.BennyHinn.org and give us your salvation praise report so we can praise God with you. You can also call that same number to talk with a precious, understanding prayer counselor if you want someone to talk and pray with you about a need or request.

God's greatest desire is an intimate relationship with His children. He wants you to know Him more deeply as you grow in your day-to-day walk with Jesus Christ: *"Being confident of this very thing, that he which hath begun a good work in you will perform it until the day of Jesus Christ"* (Philippians 1:6).

God loves you. He gave His Son for you. When you accepted Jesus Christ into your heart, you receive God's best. The most exciting adventure of all begins when you kneel at the foot of the cross. Someday your journey will end as you once again kneel at His nail-scarred feet in heaven. What a time that will be! Bill Gaither's timeless song says this so wonderfully:

> God sent His Son—they called Him Jesus;
> He came to love, heal and forgive.
> He lived and died to buy my pardon;
> An empty grave is there to prove my Savior lives.
>
> Because He lives I can face tomorrow.
> Because He lives all fear is gone.
> Because I know He holds the future,
> And life is worth the living—just because He lives.[1]

NOTES

Introduction

1. George Bennard, "The Old Rugged Cross," 1913.

Chapter 1

1. Josh McDowell, *A Ready Defense* (Nashville, TN: Thomas Nelson, 1993), 210.
2. C. S. Lewis, *Mere Christianity* (New York: HarperCollins, 2001), 51.
3. Norman Anderson, *Jesus Christ: The Witness of History* (Downers Grove, IL: InterVarsity Press, 1984), 113–114.
4. Lewis, *Mere Christianity*, 52.
5. Lewis, 52.

A Final Word

1. William J. Gaither, "Because He Lives," copyright © 1971 by William J. Gaither. All rights reserved. Used by permission.

life of unborn child.

Isa 49:1
     49:5   in . womb.
Jer 1:4 & 5   (death penalty of unborn)

Luk 1:14-15 & 41
Gen 25:21-23 sona gram - 2 nations

Lev 21:

PS 127:3-5
it's not your body.
    I cor 6:18-20 DNA. Living Soul.
your creator does.
life is the 1st Constitution of U.S.of A.

Isa 10:1 - unrighteous decrees
      Blamed in Day of Judgment.

PROV 31:8-9
PS 41 : 1-3 supernatural blessed life.

Larry Huck Atonement